D0383224

Faith Influences

Gospel Responsibilities in a Changing World

Tisa Lewis

Woman's Missionary Union
Birmingham, Alabama

Woman's Missionary Union
P. O. Box 830010
Birmingham, AL 35283-0010

For more information, visit our Web site at www.wmu.com or call 1-800-968-7301.

©2000 by Woman's Missionary Union
All rights reserved. First printing 2000
Printed in the United States of America
Woman's Missionary Union®, WMU®, Girls in Action®, and GA® are registered trademarks.

All rights reserved. No part of this publication may be reproduced, stored in a retrieval system, or transmitted in any form or by any means—electronic, mechanical, photocopying, recording, or otherwise—without the prior written permission of the publisher.

Dewey Decimal Classification: 234.23
Subject Headings: FAITH
BIBLE. N. T. ROMANS—STUDY AND TEACHING
CHRISTIAN LIFE

Scripture quotations identified NRSV are from the *New Revised Standard Version of the Bible,* Copyright ©1989 by the Division of Christian Education of the National Council of the Churches of Christ in the USA. Used by permission. All rights reserved.

Scripture quotations identified NEB are from the *New English Bible,* ©The Delegates of Oxford University Press and The Syndics of the Cambridge University Press, 1961, 1970. Used with permission.

Scripture quotations marked NKJV are from the New King James Version. Copyright ©1982 by Thomas Nelson, Inc. Used by permission. All rights reserved.

Scripture quotations identified TEV are from *Good News Bible,* Today's English Version. Old Testament: ©American Bible Society, 1976; New Testament: ©American Bible Society, 1966, 1971, 1976. Used by permission.

Design by Janell E. Young

ISBN: 1-56309-336-7
W004117•0500•5M1

In Memory of Mary Leaphart Lewis and Ruth Eskew Temples

Contents

Preface

An older graduate of the college where I teach recalls that decades ago when times were hard, students had to hope for the best when they went to the cafeteria. It seems a certain gravy was used to doctor whatever was being served, but nobody knew exactly what was *in* the gravy. It's safe to say, the ingredients were next to impossible to identify, but the students ate it anyway. After a while, the students began to call this "faith gravy" or "the substance of things hoped for, the evidence of things not seen."

Like that gravy, faith is often inexplicable. The mysterious and sometimes nebulous nature of faith frequently defies verbalization. One United States senator who seemed at a loss for words when asked to describe pornography said, "I can't tell you what it is, but I know it when I see it." Like that senator's failure to verbalize his understanding of a concept, at times the abstract quality of faith leaves us grasping for words. However, we recognize it when we see evidence of it in our lives and the lives of those who've influenced us.

Whether or not we have faith and how much of it we have is based largely on what we have experienced in our lives, good and bad. People are certainly a huge factor in the type and the degree of faith we have, as well as the frequency with which we exhibit it. These people add a dimension to our lives that encourages hope, trust, and joy; or possibly despair, mistrust, and sorrow.

Faith influences. We can see these two words in two different ways, as a simple sentence with a subject and a verb or a phrase with an adjective and a noun. Certainly our personal faith and the faith of others influence our lives in remarkable ways. Likewise, various faith influences contribute color, texture, and meaning to our lives both quantitatively and qualitatively.

Our faith influences us cognitively through our thoughts; affectively through our feelings and emotions; behaviorally through our actions; and, of course, spiritually. The presence or absence of faith affects every domain of our lives. On the other hand, every domain of our lives has tremendous influence on the type and amount of faith we possess. The 16 chapters of Romans and the 12 chapters of this book explore all of these domains in one way or another.

All along our life journeys, we meet people who serve as faith influences for us for whom we can likewise be faith influences. Paul certainly influenced and was influenced by individuals in all walks of life, Jews and Gentiles, men and women, young and old, rich and poor. By delving into Paul's letter to the Romans, we will get glimpses of these people who influenced and were influenced by his ministry. However, this little book that you are reading is not a formal, academic Bible study of the Book of Romans. Instead, it will serve as more of a look at what some of Paul's words can offer us in this changing world as we strive to live out our gospel responsibilities. We will not closely examine every verse of Romans, and we will certainly accentuate some more than others. I will quickly express my bias towards exploring verses that prompt us to action and examination of our attitudes, our values, and our beliefs. At times my examples or stories may seem a bit of a stretch when compared to Paul's words, but I pray that Christ will be illuminated in some small way in each illustration and in each person you meet in these pages.

No doubt, all of you could construct long lists of individuals whose lives and experiences have helped cause your faith to grow or to wilt. Early on, you will meet Nakia, a precocious child who is curious at best and maybe even a little irreverent at worst but nonetheless is someone who has had a huge impact on my thinking. In the 12 chapters of this book, I will introduce you to numerous other people including my students, my friends, and my family members whose faith has profoundly influenced my life. At times I will use real names, but at times I will offer a pseudonym to protect the innocent!

From the outset, I will admit that parts of Paul's letter to the Romans give me pause. But I see that as a challenge to try to more fully understand what God would have me see in those verses. My interpretations are mine alone unless I cite another source. And my interpretation is not *the* interpretation, but is merely a starting point to get the conversation going. As in my classes at Montreat College, we will ask more questions than we will answer. Rather than trying to come to conclusions on certain issues, often I will ask you to come to your own for your own reasons, not for mine and not necessarily for Paul's. Through a series of questions in every chapter we will seek to examine how words written in the first century can influence us 20 centuries later. Some of the topics we explore will be controversial ones, and if you read these chapters with friends, you may not be unanimous in your interpretations and understandings of the material. But even in our differences, the unity that we experience through the joy, love, and peace of God will move us toward the gospel responsibilities Christ commands.

As I mentioned earlier, many people have been tremendous faith influences in my life. Some of those same people had quite an influence on what you will read in these pages. If you like what you read, you have them to thank. If you don't, I'll take responsibility for that. I am indebted to Jan Turrentine for offering me the opportunity to expand into this format a series of articles on Romans that Julie Smith and I wrote several years ago in *Royal Service* (now *Missions Mosaic*). For their support, I cannot overstate my gratitude to my parents, Bobby and Joan Lewis. Sarah Ennis, my work-study student, provided helpful insights in several chapters of the manuscript. To Heather Ferguson, Susan Shaw, Marcia Flowers, and Reba Williams, I offer my appreciation for your constant ear and words of encouragement. And finally, to my students at Montreat College, I am forever grateful for your daily faith influences that have shaped the writing of these words.

TISA LEWIS

1

The Most Important Messages of All

Romans 1

Gone are the days when telephone calls come only occasionally and one at a time. A maddening series of hums and buzzes warns us that other callers are trying to get through. Few places cloister us from the ringing of cell phones and the beeping of pagers. Rings and beeps sometimes interrupt even worship services and wedding ceremonies. Most businesses today that do not depend upon computers carry the labels Antiquated and Out of Touch (they used to be known as Quaint!). Cell phones, pagers, voice mail, conference calls, email, call waiting, call forwarding, video conferencing, chat rooms—the telecommunications industry has exploded with thousands of gadgets and gizmos designed to keep us connected to each other. Our world is obsessed with staying in touch.

The world seems to be getting smaller and smaller, at least when it comes to communication. Who would have imagined that even before we moved into the twenty-first century we would have such access to technology that allows us to communicate instantaneously by computer with friends thousands of miles away and oceans apart? In the fall of 1999 I was thrilled to turn on my computer to discover an email from my friend Janie. I have known Janie since 1975, but had not had contact with her for several years. As a missionary, Janie had moved from country to country and continent to continent spreading the good news of Christ. Imagine my surprise when I suddenly "heard" via email from my old friend who had been such an important faith influence in my life. I was even more surprised and amazed that I could be sitting at my computer in North Carolina typing a message that Janie would receive within the blink of an eye. What's even more amazing is that I can communicate with her for free; not even the price of a stamp or five cents a minute is needed. God works in mysterious ways and so do computers!

We go to an awful lot of trouble and expense to be available for round-the-clock communication and conversation with people who are special to us. But if we're not careful, we will miss out on the most important messages of all: the messages of God. Many times our phones, faxes, emails, and pagers receive much more attention from us than the quiet but persistent call of God in our lives.

How does God speak to you or how do you recognize things that are of God? Three-year-old Daniel repeatedly approached his mother, distraught because God had never spoken to him. In his short lifetime he had constantly heard through Bible stories and through everyday experiences that God had spoken to this person and that person. Frustrated Daniel often said to his mother, "I listen and listen, but God has never said one word to me. What am I supposed to do?" Sometimes we are not unlike little Daniel in our fervent desire to have God tell us what to do, what to be, and what choices to make. Some of us do not get the hang of being still and knowing that God is God and can speak to us in ways that we have never imagined.

Paul's letter to the church at Rome can lead us to consider God's message and can illuminate ways we can be responsible to it faithfully, effectively, and purposefully. Our failure to respond to God's word hurts no one more than it hurts us, depriving us of the abundant life God desires for us. Determine now to pursue the presence of God in your life with a lifelong, nothing-held-back kind of commitment. Consider how God is speaking to you as you look at how God spoke to Paul.

Paul wrote Romans while he was in Corinth, toward the latter part of his career as an apostolic preacher, somewhere between A.D. 53 and 59.[1] Beverly Gaventa in *The Women's Bible Commentary* tells us that the Book of Romans as interpreted by religious leaders such as Augustine, Martin Luther, and Karl Barth has had tremendous influence on Christians in the Western world. Because most of those interpreters were male and because this letter of Paul seldom speaks directly to women, "might prompt the conclusion that Romans has little significance for the lives of women." However, as Gaventa points out, we will see several themes that serve as faith influences in women's lives.[2]

Romans comes closer than any of his other letters to being a systematic statement of Paul's faith. In Paul's introduction to the letter to the Romans he begins (vv. 1–7) with a salutation, which follows the custom in that day of naming the writer of the letter at the beginning. Today we would sign, *Sincerely, Jane* at the end of our letters, but Paul, according to customs of the first century, placed his name at the beginning, not at the end, of the letter. Notice in the first few verses of chapter 1 how many times he uses the names of Jesus or Christ. From the beginning of this letter to its end, Paul refers to Jesus as the One Who calls him.

Paul included very little of the person of Jesus in the Book of Romans. Not until approximately 15 years after the epistle to the Romans was written were the details of Jesus' life recorded in the Gospel of Mark. Mark's work closely followed the Pauline account showing how much his faith had been influenced by the writings of Paul. While this book will concentrate on the letter of Paul to the Romans, we will also examine closely Jesus' call to gospel responsibility, His admonitions to us to love God and our neighbor, that we see in the writings of Matthew, Mark, and Luke.

Paul saw his calling not as cultivator or pastor, but as a seed planter or an evangelist to non-Jews. Paul hoped to visit the church at Rome on his way to Spain, his proposed field of work. His letter announced his desire to visit the Roman Christians and to enlist their support for his Spanish mission. Seeing this as part of his purpose, Paul stressed "the universal need of salvation in Christ and the universal availability, as well as the perfection, of that salvation."[3] He clearly expresses the impartiality of God. This book will examine those words of Paul and will offer suggestions as to how we might respond to God's message as illuminated by Paul.

Responsible to take the right steps

A unique way to look at God's impartiality and Paul's emphasis on the all-inclusiveness of the gospel is by examining Clarence Jordan's *The Cotton Patch Version of Paul's Epistles*. Jordan, a scholar of New Testament Greek writing a modern-day translation of Paul's writings, sees Paul not as an aristocratic Pharisee but as a converted southerner in twentieth-century America. Try to secure a copy of *The Cotton Patch Version of Paul's Epistles* and read Clarence Jordan's humorous version. Using colloquial language Jordan helps us understand what Paul was saying to the Romans. Since in Paul's day, Rome was the military, political, and economic capital of the world, Jordan encourages us to imagine Paul addressing his letter to Christians in Washington, D.C., convincing them that the gospel of Christ is for Americans and foreigners, black and white, female and male. Without a doubt, modern-day Christians in Washington and Waycross, Birmingham and Boston, are just as called and responsible as were the first-century Christians at Rome.

In a letter Paul wrote to his fellow Christian believers at Corinth, he noted that since they were babes in the faith, he could give them only the milk of Christian thinking (1 Cor. 3:1–2). On the other hand, Paul obviously believed that the Christians in Rome were ready for solid food. How else would he have been able to broach such an important and colossal issue as creation's relationship to the Creator?[4] If theology is the truth about God and God's relationship to God's creation, Romans is indeed boldly theological.

Christ's Faith Influence

After Paul identifies himself as the sender of the letter in verse 1, he gives us what Paul Achtemeier sees as the central theme in Romans 1:2–4. What do you think the theme is? While some insist that the theme of Romans is the doctrine of justification by faith, Achtemeier says the central theme of Romans "is the plan God is pursuing to extend his gracious lordship to all people by his act in Christ."[5] (See Phil. 2:9–11.) Paul associated himself with his readers by saying that they, too, were called to belong to Christ, to be the people of God. These people were not perfect, but they had responded to God's leading and were progressing in the right direction. Like them, we have not yet arrived but are taking the right steps and are still searching. Thus, a call to salvation is a responsibility to service. What responsibilities have you taken lately that show you are progressing in God's call upon your life?

Paul repeated his idea that the gospel was universal when he used both a Greek greeting, *charis,* or "grace," and the Greek word *eirene* to express the idea of the normal Hebrew greeting, *shalom,* or "peace" (Rom. 1:7). Paul combined Hebrew and Greek ideas in his message of God's love and caring for all races and nationalities.[6] You will see this continuously throughout the Book of Romans. He was convinced that God's word of grace must be available to all, not by our own merits or accomplishments but by the mercy of God.

Questions for personal reflection

1. What do you think is the major idea in Romans 1:2–4?
2. What responsibilities has God called you to?

Responsible to pray and listen

With the exception of the letter to the Galatians, Paul generally expressed gratitude to his readers (Rom. 1:8). He let the Roman Christians know that he had been praying for them (Rom. 1:9–10). Look at your intercessory prayer list and reflect on your own commitment to intercede for others. This kind of unceasing intercessory prayer is a mark of all who have received and accepted Christ and the gospel responsibility that comes with that gift.

Like Paul, when we come in contact with those for whom we have prayed, those previous prayers profoundly affect our response to those individuals. In verse 9 we see that Paul was quite dedicated to those for whom he was interceding and prayed without ceasing. Our prayers are not only a means of communicating with God, but they also serve as personal reminders to keep in our consciousness those who are in need of support.

Prayer often helps us organize our thoughts and moves our concerns from ourselves to others. Through speaking to God we are also speaking to ourselves, and in some mysterious way God speaks to us through our own thoughts and words.

Martin Luther King Jr. conveyed a similar idea when he prayed, "Speak to us, dear God, so that we can hear You, and thereby ourselves."[7] Similarly Robert Coles who has interviewed many children to get their ideas on God relays what 9-year-old Avram believed about the voice of God. Maybe Avram's explanation could help little Daniel, mentioned previously. Avram says, "It's not His voice—I mean, He doesn't speak to us when we pray; we speak to ourselves. But it's Him telling us what to say—to tell ourselves."[8] We just have to be open to the leading of the Holy Spirit, free our minds of interference, and allow God to invade our thoughts and fill us with holiness.

You have probably had the experience of praying something or writing something that seemed to be not of you. You may have asked, "Where did that come from or how did I know that?" I am convinced that when people come to mind whom we have not thought of lately, that may be God's way of telling us to take some time to be in contact with that person. Maybe we cannot get that person off of our minds because the Holy Spirit is prompting us to act. The mysteries of God are unfathomable, marvelous, and bring us closer to the kingdom of God on Earth if only we will take time to listen and give God room in our minds and lives.

Paul saw his upcoming visit to the Christians at Rome as an occasion for sharing (Rom. 1:11–12). Recognizing their maturity in the faith, Paul wanted his readers to know that they had something to offer. Their faith could strengthen and inform him. As in Luke 6:38, the exchange involves both giving and receiving.

A couple of years ago I attended a gathering of Christian educators where we discussed the topic of listening to the voices of others. A part of the discussion centered on the fact that some Christians get upset when others seem not to listen to or hear their voices, particularly those who may disagree with them or who may have different perspectives. The speaker at the gathering reminded us that often some people do not want to listen to people who believe their perspective is the only perspective, whose arrogance closes their ears to valuable, enlightening information that others have to offer. He said that only when we come to the discussion table with humility and charity should we expect to be heard. Only when Christians are willing to listen are they able to teach and preach effectively. Others will listen to us if we listen carefully to them. Who are people you need to hear this week? Think how you can be a more effective listener so that you can share mutual faith in God.

Questions for personal reflection

1. How do you think Paul prayed?
2. What advice would Paul give you about improving your prayer life?
3. Are there relationships in which you need to listen more than you talk?

Responsible to be all we can be

Paul's obligation was not just to the Christians in the church at Rome but "to the civilized and to the savage, to the educated and to the ignorant" (Rom. 1:14). Until he had completed his commission from God, Paul would not be satisfied. He recognized the odds against him, but he saw faith as being active rather than passive.

Like Paul, we must do something in response to our faith. We are accountable. Reread verse 12 and then list the actions you have taken this month that reflect accountability. Reread verse 15. Paul was called to preach to the Romans, and he wanted to do that with all his might. What do you feel God has called you to do? Are you determined to do it with all your might, your energy, and your total personality? Spend a few moments in meditation now. Listen to God as He calls you to serve. Write down what God impels you to do, so that you can remember this call. Continue to listen to God's "still, small voice" every day.

In verses 16 and 17 we see the radical grace that God offers us. Verse 16 says, "For I am not ashamed of the gospel; it is the power of God for salvation to everyone who has faith, to the Jew first and also to the Greek" (NRSV). At the end of a course on faith development, one of my best students, who for nearly 4 years had exhibited wonderful Christlike qualities to everyone she met, was giving a presentation. All her years as a student, Cassie was well liked and was known and admired for her volunteer work at the homeless shelter and with Habitat for Humanity. She shocked everyone in the class when she stood up and said, "I do not call myself a Christian and do not want to be identified with anything that is blatantly Christian." Cassie proceeded to tell us why.

She had grown up in a church that was quite judgmental toward people of other races and toward people who were not Christians. Several members of her church were heavily involved in the Ku Klux Klan and had even burned a cross in the front yard of her best friend who was a Jew. They had also written slanderous comments in black spray paint on the white vinyl siding of the house of her uncle who was gay. In the name of Christ these church members had chastised and made fun of people who were not like them, and Cassie was ashamed to be associated with those people who called themselves Christians. These early faith influences in her life, while isolated and extreme, had colored her impression of Christians.

In her presentation she went on to say how much she loved Jesus and tried to be like Him, but the actions of her fellow church members in the name of Christ had turned her off to the point that she wanted nothing to do with their faith. Obviously these experiences did not give Cassie an excuse to be ashamed of the gospel, but they did help us to understand how she felt. How might we be positive faith influences in the lives of people like Cassie and help them know the radical grace of God? Are we reflecting Christlikeness in ways that attract others to Christianity rather than repel them and cause them to be ashamed of association with the gospel?

Responsible for our attitudes and actions

Verses 18–32 present Paul's description of God's displeasure over ungodly people. How it must disappoint God when we turn away and engage in sinful behavior, think selfish thoughts, and possess ungodly attitudes. As the Creator of all creation, God holds the sinful creature "without excuse" (v. 20 NRSV). So many things that we participate in do not glorify God and cause a disunion in our relationship to God and others in our lives.

Often we see sin as those things that we actively engage in, acts that we commit that separate us from God. We all know what these sins are and quickly recognize them. Most of us would have no problem listing these overt sins that we are guilty of, that we observe in the media, and that have plagued our friends and families. No doubt sin does include all of these things. However, sometimes we do not acknowledge that sin also includes those things that we fail to do, acts that we omit. We often justify our acts of omission by saying that at least we are not engaging in immoral activities that hurt ourselves and others, taking the self-righteous perspective of the Pharisee in Luke 18:11 who said, "'God, I thank you that I am not like other people.'" In the process of being self-righteous, much of God's work goes undone and many of God's children suffer as a result.

Romans 1:23 explains how the creatures' reaction to their Creator has been idolatrous. Paul attacked Gentile idolatry, as Israel's idolatry was prohibited in Deuteronomy 4:15–19. As in Psalm 106:19–20, a reference to the golden calf, humans ceased to honor and give thanks to God and instead looked to other images.[9] In our desire to master our circumstances, we sometimes have a religious pride where we see ourselves as Lord and presume to know God's will and possess God's favor. How arrogant to think that I have the market on God's will and that God looks on me with a special pleasure! This is the height of selfishness. Nearly all of the seven deadly sins of anger, pride, avarice or greed, sloth, gluttony, lust, and envy, many of which are the same sins that Paul lists at the end of chapter 1, involve some form of selfishness. These seven specific sins that were pointed out by the monastic movement are more apparent in the lives of many of us than we would like to admit.

Idolatry, then, may take many forms, including wealth, nationalism, racism, sexism, religiosity, or any pleasure whereby we might try to pursue our own desires in complete independence from God. Thus, idolatry is the substitution of anything other than the Creator as Lord. This desire can eat away at us and ultimately destroy us. If you have anything in your life that you know is more important than serving God, are you willing to give it up today? Prepare a list of changes you can make in your life so that God is foremost in all you do.

Romans 1:24–32 divides the list of vices between the *sensual*, showing defilement of the body, and the *anti-social*, showing defilement of the human spirit.[10] Stop now and pick out the sensual vices. Not only are these people doing these wrongs, but they are also doing them with the approval of society (v. 32). Paul may be implying that encouraging others to commit such sins is actually worse than committing the sin. Ask God to reveal any of your actions that may cause others to sin.

Paul made it clear here that we are accountable to use God's creation in the way it was ordered. Abuse of that creation, including our own bodies, is an insult to the Creator. This abuse could certainly include the destruction of natural resources, but Paul mainly focused on the vices involving relationships. God's punishment or wrath for this sin is not overt or direct punishment. Instead, God will let us have our own way (v. 26). We punish ourselves by rejecting the Creator as Lord.

Responsible without excuse

We can quite easily point out the idolatry, sin, and selfishness of others. We can quickly make others accountable without accepting that accountability ourselves. However, exercising discipline and putting ourselves under the lordship of Christ will open us up to grace and protect us from wrath. Discipline, even in the form of controlling our tongues or our diets, will keep us from ruining our lives, God's creation. By listening to and becoming accountable to God, we can become all we are meant to be in the eyes of the Creator.

In March 1993, the blizzard of the century hit my little town. I can remember measuring 27 inches of snow on my back deck. That's a lot of snow for North Carolina, particularly during my college's spring break. The wind was so strong and so sustained that the 4-foot icicles off the eaves of my house were shaped like commas. Many people were unprepared for the isolation that they experienced because of impassable roads, interrupted telephone service, and no electrical power. All means of communication were suspended for some, particularly those who did not have battery operated radios. Maggie Johnson, living alone, found herself in this predicament and said that during that time, God spoke to her in a way that she had never experienced. Fierce winds blew all around Maggie's home causing whiteout conditions and obscuring her view of the nearest neighbor. As she sat watching the flames of an open fire, her only source of heat, she said that she communicated with God on an incredible level with no possible interruption from any other outside source. The encounter was profound, just Maggie and God, in near silence except for the gusting wind.

Numerous people who found themselves in a similar situation during the blizzard of 1993 echoed this woman's experience. While this circumstance was unique and extreme, it had a tremendous faith influence on those who lived through it. Unfortunately it sometimes takes a powerful blizzard to make us be still and listen to the voice of God. But that voice is always accessible, calling us to gospel responsibility.

Questions for personal reflection

1. Are there areas of your life that you still control? Why do you think you are reluctant to relinquish this control to God?
2. How, when, and where do you most often hear God speaking to you?

[1]Clifton J. Allen, ed., *The Broadman Bible Commentary* (Nashville: Broadman Press, 1970), 10:153.
[2]Beverly Roberts Gaventa, "Romans," in *The Women's Bible Commentary,* ed. Carol A. Newsom and Sharon H. Ringe (Louisville, KY: Westminster/John Knox Press, 1992), 315.
[3]George Arthur Buttrick, ed., *The Interpreter's Bible* (Nashville: Abingdon Press, 1978), 9:359.
[4]Paul J. Achtemeier, *Romans*, vol. in *Interpretation: A Bible Commentary for Teaching and Preaching* (Louisville, KY: John Knox Press, 1985), 2.
[5]Ibid., 22.
[6]Ibid., 30.
[7]Robert Coles, *The Spiritual Life of Children* (Boston: Houghton Mifflin Company, 1990), 77.
[8]Ibid., 76.
[9]Ernst Kasemann, *Commentary on Romans* (Grand Rapids, MI: William B. Eerdmans, 1978), 45.
[10]Allen, *Broadman Bible Commentary,* 10:171.

2

Responsibility for Our Sin

Romans 2:1 to 3:20

Twelve-year-old Nakia was disturbed at what she had heard called Christian all of her life. "I'll bet you Jesus sometimes gets sick and tired of having His name tacked on to every little thing we want to carry a lot of weight or when we really want to get our own selfish point across. Don't you think we ought to be more careful how we throw around that word *Christian* in our sinful little lives?"

Little Nakia calls it the way she sees it. She will surface periodically and will make some bold comments and ask some pointed questions. Maybe your children are asking some of the same questions Nakia has asked, especially questions that concern our relationships to God and our brothers and sisters.

The previous chapter dealt with the universal need for and availability of salvation in Christ. In Romans 1, Paul explained that the root of sin is the substitution of anything other than the Creator as Lord; and as punishment, God lets us have our way with our idolatrous natures. However, the story does not end there. Read Romans 2. You may want to read this in several translations. Note especially verses 1 and 2.

20
Accountable for all the things we do

"Do you, my friend, pass judgment on others?" From the outset, Paul asks a question in Romans 2:1 (TEV) that we must obviously answer in the affirmative. Yes, indeed, we are all guilty of passing judgment on others. Compare this verse with Luke 6:37. Somehow, blasting the faults of others subtly gives us a sense of superiority. We think if we lower the worth of others, our own sense of worth increases. When we fail, sin, or make mistakes, we quickly try to cover things up, give reasons, or make excuses; however, we immediately chastise others who make the same plea. Sadly, Christians are often the first to shoot their wounded.

Questions for personal reflection

1. When have you observed or experienced this "shooting the wounded"?
2. Why do you suppose people condemn others of the exact sins they themselves commit? Have you ever done this? How? When?

Many times in judging others we may do so in the absence of the full truth. The story is told of Margaret who after hours of Christmas shopping goes to the massive food court of a local mall. She is inundated by entrées calling out to her: egg rolls, pizzas, stuffed potatoes, salads, and sandwiches of all descriptions. She decides on the Chinese special, pays for her meal, and scouts out a place to sit.

The seating is limited, but finally locating an empty chair, she settles down to enjoy her stir-fried vegetables and chicken. Realizing that she forgot to pick up some sweet and sour sauce, she leaves the table to go back to the condiment counter. When she returns to her chair, Margaret is shocked to discover that a rather disheveled, hunched older man has seated himself at her table and is devouring her meal. Irate, she scolds the startled man saying that she cannot believe that he would have the gall to eat something that someone else has paid for, something that did not belong to him. The embarrassed man quickly leaves the table without saying a word.

Margaret mutters under her breath to the couple at the table next to her, complaining that all anyone is looking for these days is a handout from hardworking people like herself. Determined not to be defeated, she sits down at the half-eaten platter and suddenly spies out of the corner of her eye a Chinese special sitting on the table next to her, her Chinese special. She had mistaken the disheveled man's meal for her own.

Romans 2:2 reminds us that God alone judges according to the truth. God alone sees all and knows all the facts. When Christians judge others, we exhibit pride in ourselves that is both absurd and tragic. Even if we sometimes consider ourselves *good*, we may allow our goodness to betray us into a sense of self-satisfaction. We seem to feel that if we can portray others as being worse than ourselves, we can feel justified and may even feel we can escape punishment. However, we are accountable for our judgment of others.

Questions for personal reflection

1. Have you ever said unkind things about others so that you appear to be a better person than they are?
2. How have you judged somebody this week for his or her lifestyle?

No doubt, in chapter 2 Paul expresses his theology, his understanding of God, and how God relates to people. I must admit that this chapter gives me pause when I try to understand how failed responsibility on one hand corresponds with forgiveness on the other. Is salvation an all or nothing reward, or are there degrees of reward based on our doing good?

Even as we judge others, God is quite patient. This passage tells us that God's delay of judgment gives every sinner opportunity to repent, not a chance to do more evil. Here Paul plainly says that the delay of punishment is temporary, and a day of reckoning is a reality. Verses 6–8 have always confounded me, in much the same way as the second half of Matthew 25 that I will discuss later. I confessed this to the students in one of my classes as an honest confession and to prompt some discussion, and one of them told me I was failing to see what Paul was plainly stating and was trying to avoid responsibility. But I am still puzzled by how God's judgment works. This New Testament teaching merely reiterates the Old Testament conviction that we see in Amos 5:18 and other places.[1] Compare Romans 2:4–6 with Amos 5:18. How are they similar? Notice references to the "day of the Lord," or the day of judgment. How do you believe God judges sinners? How does forgiveness of sin through Christ's sacrifice enter into this discussion?

Strong words about our gospel responsibility to do good works and to care for those in need also appear in Matthew 25:41–46. Recently in my church a woman prefaced her reading of this passage by saying she was not comfortable with what it had to say. I appreciated her honesty and understood her discomfort. What do you do with these words we are told Jesus said? I don't know about you, but I am too often awfully guilty of not doing "to one of the least of these." Verses 45–46 (NASB) say that those of us who "did not do it to one of the least of these . . . will go away into eternal punishment." Clearly good works are crucial and necessary in our gospel responsibility.

At times, some Christians have seen justification by faith in opposition to any emphasis on the value of good works. But actually the contrast is more apparent than real. (Study Rom. 2:6–11 carefully.) Justification is *by* faith but judgment is *according to* works. Good works are not legalistic conformity to an external code of ethics but are an expression of a heartfelt spirituality. What does God say in verse 10 about rewards? Is this verse referring to earthly rewards or heavenly rewards?

The question of motive often arises when we seek to do good works. Are we seeking to gain God's favor and avoid God's wrath? Are we trying to win someone's approval? Are we attempting to satisfy our own conscience? Or are we simply doing the right thing because it's the right thing to do? The larger question may be, Are we looking for an external reward or is the reward in the act itself? We use the word *altruism* to describe a beneficent act performed by an individual expecting nothing in return. Is this possible, or are we always looking to gain something from the good works that we do?

As Christians we should constantly question our motives for our behaviors. In T. S. Eliot's *Murder in the Cathedral*, one quote epitomizes this idea of motive: "The last temptation is the greatest treason: To do the right deed for the wrong reason." We need quite a bit of altruism and maturity not to expect thanks or recognition for our good deeds, for our beneficent acts. Most of us want at least a pat on the back for a job well done, for volunteer service, or for being neighborly. We get upset when people seem ungrateful for our donations of time and money. But shouldn't the good act itself be enough?

Martin Luther said that faith "is a most vivid, active, and busy thing, which cannot help doing good deeds all the time."[2] You might, then, see *faith* more accurately as an action word, like a verb, instead of a naming word, like a noun. We are not judged by the opinions we hold but by what we do and the kind of lives we lead. (Read James 2:14–26.) What changes do you need to make in your life so that others can see outward signs of your inner change? Eternal life is God's gift, not our achievement.

I once asked my students in a Christian education class to play a little game with me. I said, "Suppose eternal life did not exist, that this was not a reward for being a Christian and trying to follow Christ's teachings. Would you still seek to live a Christlike life? Would being Christlike be a reward in itself?" One of my students responded that the only reason he was a Christian was to gain "fire insurance," to escape the flames of hell and the wrath of God. He saw no other reason for being a Christian.

Contrast this student's attitude with another student's, Allison's. Allison was required to work 180 hours in a human services-related area in order to satisfy the requirements for an internship. She absolutely dreaded this and told me she could not wait until she had finished putting in her time. But something divine happened in the process of fulfilling the requirements for the course.

The internship Allison chose committed her to being the primary caregiver 8 hours a day for 7-year-old Jeremy who had cerebral palsy. Fear of the unknown and apprehension about working with a special needs child overwhelmed her. But after about a week of caring for this precious child, Allison became quite attached. Every day when Allison arrived at Jeremy's house, his eyes would light up. He would ask her how her morning had been and what new and exciting things she had seen on the ride to his house. After a warm greeting Jeremy would then want to know what new adventure they would take that day.

It didn't take long for Allison to decide that even when her 180 hours were completed, she would maintain a relationship with Jeremy. She loved his company and the way he brightened her day. For several months after the internship was completed, Allison and Jeremy enjoyed hours together learning from each other and discovering God's creation until Jeremy's weak little body drew in its last breath with Allison at his side. While Allison certainly mourned Jeremy's death, she also gave thanks to God that this priceless opportunity to serve and be served had come her way.

What began as a motive to satisfy a course requirement turned into something much different. At the end of her senior year, Allison told me that her time with Jeremy had helped her to see that being Christlike was a reward in itself. She thought a lot about that question we had raised in class. She concluded that she was a Christian not just because she would go to heaven but because she was beginning to understand that Christlikeness was the lifestyle she preferred and that the world seemed like a better place when she sought to live as Christ lived.

Allison's faith had been dramatically influenced by her relationship with Jeremy. We serve God through good deeds to others out of gratitude to God for the marvelous free gift God has given us! We want to serve God because we love God. Since God first loved us, we return that love and share it with the world.

To be doers, not hearers only

In Romans 2:12–16, Paul speaks repeatedly of the "law," or the Torah. In basic form, the law referred to the Ten Commandments (Deut. 5; Ex. 20:1–20). However, scholars usually acknowledge that the law includes the Bible's first five books, often called the Pentateuch, which the Jews believe Moses wrote. Another meaning of the law may include "all the laws and interpretations of laws which had been developed by the Jews after the Pentateuch had finally been put together (this is believed to have been about the fourth or fifth century B.C.)."[3] All definitions of the law include "both regulations which refer to moral conduct; e.g. 'Thou shall not kill' . . . and those which deal with matters of ritual, e.g. the laws about the kinds of food which a Jew should or should not eat. . . . Paul is largely concerned with the laws relating to moral behaviour."[4]

Paul says that each person will be judged by what that person actually knows of the law (v. 12). God will take into account the opportunities we have had. That is, "'to whom much has been given, much will be required'" (Luke 12:48 NRSV). The law really belongs only to the one who practices it, and only the doers of the law shall be accounted righteous (Rom. 2:13). We are accountable to be doers and not simply hearers of the word (James 1:22–25).

In Romans 2:14–15, Paul emphasizes that moral insight may come from more than one source. John Calvin said, "There never was a nation so barbarous or inhuman that it did not regulate life by some form of law. . . . There are certain original conceptions of right which are imprinted on the hearts of men by nature."[5] However, the person who operates from a higher law will have an advantage over the one "who is prompted only by a sense of natural decency."[6]

Theorists who study moral behavior and development say that people who function at lower stages of development are moral so as to avoid punishment or guilt. Those operating at higher stages of moral reasoning and development are moral because of an internal compulsion to be so, to do the good. Christ living within us motivates us without our needing legislation or some external authority such as a police officer or an authoritarian leader.

Philosophers for centuries have often debated if doing good helps us to know the good or whether knowing the good compels us to do the good. Of course, much of this depends on your definition of *know.* According to Aristotle, by doing just acts, we become just. In Allison's case, she seemed to know the good better after doing the good with Jeremy. At least in her case, she understood the good better and saw clearly the reason for serving as Christ would have her serve.

Another example of this involves the experiences of my friend Heather Ferguson's youth group. Every summer she organizes a trip to some area of the country that is in need of services that her youth can provide. These youth actually raise money to pay for the supplies that they will use and for the lodging and food that they will need.

Each youth is assigned to work with a group of people he or she has never met. Groups of six people of different denominations are assigned to a home, and each group member is encouraged to get to know the residents of the home they are repairing or renovating. Some of the services they render include building porches and steps, repairing roofs, replacing floors, hanging drywall, painting, and installing storm doors and windows. Initially many of the youth are reluctant to participate and some are even forced by their parents to take part. One young man, Will, moaned and complained to his parents for weeks before the day of departure to Webster County in West Virginia. Finally he agreed to go on the trip and to make the best of it. His mother now says that he had a spiritual awakening as a result of his experience. Through his doing the good, Will gained confidence and acquired new skills, realized how much he had in common with people of other denominations, and received more than he could ever give. Not only did he influence the faith of the residents with whom he worked; they influenced his faith. Being Christlike taught him Christlikeness.

In serving others whom we consider to be less fortunate, we must be careful not to take an elitist attitude, to think that we are blessed and those with whom we are working are not. One indigent woman in Appalachia anticipating the arrival of missionaries voiced her opinion of the many well-intentioned missionaries who had served her community previously. She said, "If you believe that you are coming just to improve my life, then you can go home. If you believe that I also have something to teach you, then let's roll up our sleeves and work together." Knowing the good does not give us license to think that we are elite. With charity must come humility. But again, as Luke reminds us, "'To whom much has been given, much will be required.'" Doing the good influences our faith, reinforces our gospel responsibility, and intrinsically motivates us to love others as God loves us.

Questions for personal reflection

1. What condemnation does Romans 2:1–3 give?
2. How does Romans 2:4 show that God reaches out to us?
3. What is your response to Matthew 5:41–46 concerning punishment for not taking care of those who need help?
4. What does Romans 2:12–16 tell you about the law?

Read carefully Romans 2:17–24. Paul's reference to the blind leaders of the blind (v. 19) echoes Jesus' words in Matthew 15:14 and 23:16. The aimless fumblings of prideful individuals cannot direct helpless ignorance.

These "blind" leaders have no vision because they have no light. Only the word of God illuminates the darkness, a common biblical metaphor (Isa. 9:2; 2 Cor. 4:6).[7] Those who hypocritically claim to be leaders and teachers will be held accountable when they do not practice what they preach (Rom. 2:20–24).

In my classes I constantly talk about our responsibility to love God and our neighbors. Whenever natural disasters such as hurricanes and floods take the lives of people or destroy homes and livelihoods, before class begins we remember in prayer those who have suffered extreme loss. This is a good thing, and this is easy. Taking the step from teaching the good to modeling the good is more difficult, and I am constantly guilty of not practicing what I preach, of not putting feet on my prayers. And even when I feel convicted of not serving those who could use my help, I am still lazy, too often using my leisure time to selfishly pursue hobbies that I enjoy or treating myself to a luxury that I don't really need. Often my faith looks dead to my students and to myself. I have to continually shake myself awake from my comfortable existence and ask for motivation to do the good, to reflect God's love, to take gospel responsibility.

Many of us may think we are excused from Paul's admonition in these verses by saying that we are not leaders or we are not teachers, thus exempt from this gospel responsibility. However, all of us have influence over someone whether we are parents or are just an adult a child is observing in the grocery store. Deuteronomy 6:1–9 explains clearly how our faith can influence those in our lives. Our lives are constantly an open book, whether intentional or not, and our faith and light or the lack thereof affect people around us in ways we may never imagine. Jesus calls us to be faith influences day by day when in the Great Commission of Matthew 28:18–20 He commands us to be light to others in much the same way that we read in the Deuteronomy passage. We are all teachers and leaders.

Questions for personal reflection

1. Compare Matthew 15:14 and 23:16 to Romans 2:19. How are they alike? Put the message of these verses in your own words. Explain, "The aimless fumblings of prideful individuals cannot direct helpless ignorance."
2. Read Isaiah 9:2 and 2 Corinthians 4:6 and compare their truths to those in Romans 2.
3. If you are a leader or a teacher, what implications do you find for your own life in verses 20–24? Give some examples of Christians not practicing what they preach. What is the solution to this problem?

Paul further admonishes this hypocrisy in his reference to circumcision, where he contrasts appearance and reality (vv. 25–29). My college's motto is *Esse Quam Videri*, "to be rather than to seem." We constantly evaluate whether or not we are the institution we say we are and think we are. External facades and who we profess we are as a college are not the essence of a Christian institution. We can erect crosses and build chapels proclaiming our Christ-centeredness all day long; but if we treat students, our co-workers, and our neighbors badly, our message is not only inaccurate but also a slap in the face of Christianity. We must back up banners, advertisements, and mottoes with genuine attempts at gospel responsibility. Prospective students and parents want to know if we are truly who we claim to be, at least, if we are trying to be who we say we are.

External signs of our faith such as circumcision, baptism, and even attending church are not sufficient substitutes for our active participation in the life of faith. Sometimes those outside the church act in a more Christian spirit than those who claim proudly to be church members (v. 26). God requires a circumcision of the heart (Phil. 3:3). Clarence Jordan, writing with that southern 1960s perspective, says, "For a Christian is not one who makes a show of it, nor is his church membership for status purposes." He adds that a person is a Christian "who is one on the inside, whose membership is of the heart—something spiritual and not mechanical—and who seeks not the approval of society but of God."[8] Paul Achtemeier states, "God calls to responsibility rather than privilege, to a task rather than to a status."[9]

Often we are guilty of using the adjective *Christian* to give our ideas or our motives credibility and to raise the status of what we have to say, even if our motives are selfish. Even at age 12, as noted at the beginning of this chapter, Nakia was beginning to recognize the difference in being and seeming to be. When I was in graduate school I was puzzled at an advertisement that I read for a "Christian" aerobics class. Did this mean that certain movements and exercises would not be taught, that a particular type of music would or would not be played, that the instructor was a Christian, that Scripture and prayer would be a part of the sessions, or that only professing Christians would be admitted? Is a "Christian" college one that requires students to take Bible classes and attend chapel or one that encourages students to love God and neighbor and to live as Christ would live? Often we talk about "Christian" values when we are really referring to white, middle-class preferences. We often attach the adjective *Christian* to an activity or an institution to increase its standing, almost in an arrogant sort of way, to say that this is better than and more privileged than a different and more inferior activity or institution. Like Nakia, sometimes I wonder if Christ is pleased to have His name associated with some of the things that we label Christian. In our desire to set ourselves, our ideas, and our institutions apart, we often come across as self-righteous and "holier-than-thou." The faith influence that this has on people contemplating Christianity may not be so positive.

Tom Beaudoin picks up on this idea in his book, *Virtual Faith: The Irreverent Spiritual Quest of Generation X*. Here he describes the perceptions of many Generation Xers, those people born sometime between the early 1960s and the early 1980s, who are beginning to question much of what they see being called Christian. Growing up weary of the hypocrisy that they have observed and experienced in organized religion, many of them see most churches being too exclusive and self-serving. While polls show that nearly every Generation Xer is interested in religion, many of them are skeptical about what churches can offer. Jesus is a very positive figure for them, and these Xers are interested in learning more about Him. But they see Jesus almost becoming a victim at the hands of organized religion, and many of their ideas are reflected in pop culture such as in their music, their poetry, their dress, their religious icons, and the spirituality that they choose to practice. These Xers identify with Jesus and want Him in their lives, but not necessarily in the same ways that they have seen reflected in some exclusive, pretentious, judgmental, and appearance-oriented practices.[10]

While we may to tempted to write off these Xers as immature, uninformed, rebellious individuals with a chip on their shoulders, perhaps we might listen to some of their constructive criticism about being rather than seeming to be, about circumcision of the heart rather than external signs of faith. Beaudoin, himself an Xer, points out that many of his generation are rightfully critical of some traditions. Having observed the abuse of religious authority by some teachers, preachers, and even politicians, many Xers are tempted to abandon tradition at all costs. One of Beaudoin's purposes in *Virtual Faith* is to help his generation discover and embrace what tradition has to offer. Contrasting tradition with traditionalism he picks up on Jaroslav Pelikan's idea and says, "Tradition is 'the living faith of the dead.' Traditionalism is the 'dead faith of the living,' as is all too familiar to Xers."[11] If tradition says that our hair must be a certain length and that women are inferior to men, Xers have little use for it. However, if tradition says that we must take Jesus seriously and love as God loves us, then Xers say let's get on with it.

Responsible for a covenant relationship: Romans 3:1–20

In a covenant relationship, two parties pledge something to each other. Israel promised to obey God's will (Ex. 19:8) and God promised to hold Israel as God's own people (Ex. 19:5–6). Even when Israel broke her end of the bargain, God remained faithful. Read carefully Romans 3:1–4. How do verses 3–4 apply to your life? God does not mean for us to take advantage of His merciful nature and sin just so we can be forgiven. Paul vehemently responded that evildoers universally will be condemned. Read verses 5–8 and note how Paul explains this truth.

Here Jews are in no better favor than the Gentiles. Read verses 9–18. The collection of verses from the Psalms and Isaiah in verses 10–18 makes use of parts of the human body. These verses along with verse 23 illustrate the notion of sin as the defilement of self and society and remove any notion that anyone might be exempt from sin. Here Paul says the law makes clear our condemnation. While the law shows us our duty, we cannot be saved by what we do. Does this mean that we cannot also be damned by what we do? Sin and judgment are serious affairs, but as we see in the next chapter, grace and redemption bring us hope.

Questions for personal reflection

1. How do the verses in Romans 2:25–29 compare to Philippians 3:3? What does "circumcision of the heart" mean?
2. Explain in your own words Achtemeier's quote, "God calls to responsibility rather than privilege, to a task rather than to a status."
3. What condemnation awaits evildoers?
4. Name the parts of the body in Romans 3:10–18. How are they used to illustrate a biblical principle for living?
5. Read Romans 3:19–20. How does God's law help convict you of sin? What is the role of the Holy Spirit, as you read Scriptures that point out your sins? What can you do to show repentance?

[1]George Arthur Buttrick, ed., *The Interpreter's Bible* (Nashville: Abingdon Press, 1954), 9:407.
[2]Ibid., 408.
[3]Ernest Best, *The Letter of Paul to the Romans* (London: Cambridge University Press, 1967), 27.
[4]Ibid.
[5]Clifton J. Allen, ed., *The Broadman Bible Commentary* (Nashville: Broadman Press, 1970), 10:175.
[6]Buttrick, *Interpreter's Bible*, 9:412.
[7]Ibid., 414–15.
[8]Clarence Jordan, *The Cotton Patch Version of Paul's Epistles* (New York: Association Press, 1968), 19.
[9]Paul J. Achtemeier, *Romans*, vol. in *Interpretation: A Bible Commentary for Teaching and Preaching* (Louisville, KY: John Knox Press, 1985), 53.

[10]Tom Beaudoin, *Virtual Faith: The Irreverent Spiritual Quest of Generation X* (San Francisco: Jossey-Bass Publishers, 1998).
[11]Jaroslav Pelikan, *The Vindication of Tradition* (New Haven: Yale University Press, 1984), 65, quoted in Beaudoin, *Virtual Faith,* 152.

3

Hope in a Changing World

Romans 3:21 to 5:11

Nakia was distraught over hearing again and again that "the world is going to hell in a handbasket." She had constantly heard people talking about how awful the world is and how bad people are. She says, "I am so tired of people complaining about the world. Sure, bad things happen, but there are a lot of good people around doing some pretty good things. If these other folks, some who say they are Christians, think things are so miserable, why don't they do something about it? Any donkey can kick down a barn. We need a few builders. Besides, what is a handbasket anyway?"

Does our faith in God, established through Jesus Christ, allow us to do away with the law? This is one of the questions Paul asked and answered, using a diatribe (critical) style in Romans 3:21 to 5:11. This passage brings hope to individuals who recognize their sinful, idolatrous natures, who look for some sign of optimism in a changing world. The previous chapter dealt with our responsibility for the sin in our lives; this chapter deals with how God has provided a way for us to maintain a divine relationship through faith and grace even when we continue to sin.

The gift of grace and redemption

On December 31, 1999, the world waited in anticipation of what Y2K would bring. Many people had prepared for the worst, gathering canned food, bottled water, miles of toilet paper, and rolls of cash just in case computer systems failed and chaos erupted. Some people in the mountains near my town bought guns, stocked their arsenals, and barricaded their homes to ensure that what they had so carefully gathered was protected from scavengers who might not have prepared so well. Others were more optimistic about what a new century would bring. On that New Year's Eve I attended a party at a fellow church member's home, and one of the guests reflected that optimism. She said, "Imagine what would happen if everyone in the world were hopeful at the same time." We have much to be hopeful for, and Paul gives us that good word in the following passages.

Look at Romans 3:21 in several translations. The word *now* (3:21), used so often in Romans, points to the transition between the promises of God as seen in the law and the fulfillment of those promises through Jesus. Sin, or missing the mark, causes us to fall short, but we do not fall from God's grace.[1] Faith in Jesus Christ, the Fulfillment of the promise, allows us to be put right with God. In Romans 3:22–23,29, Paul speaks of every person in the universe (called a "theme of universality"), since all of us have ruptured our relationship to God through our idolatry. We are in need of what Christ has to offer. Only grace makes us right with God, nothing else.

This free gift of grace is an act of God, initiated by God, showing the true nature of God.[2] We can understand this truth through the analogy of a slave being auctioned in the marketplace. When I lived in Charleston, South Carolina, I often visited the market where slaves were once auctioned to the highest bidder. These slaves, many of whom were just children, were often separated from their families, never to see them again. Growing up as a privileged white girl secure and protected by laws forbidding these practices, I could not imagine the terror and uncertainty that those slaves must have felt. But try to put yourself on the auction block, all alone and vulnerable to the one who buys you. Christ sees us, the frightened, ragged slaves who are confined by chains, never having tasted freedom. Imagine how you would feel if a wealthy gentleman is bidding on you at this moment. As the auction begins, the persistent gentleman continues to bid on you until he succeeds in the purchase, just as he has bid his last dollar. Fully expecting to be dragged off the block by the new master, you are awestruck when the gentleman, who has spent all his money, unfastens the chain and says, "You are free to go. Go in peace."

Not only are we free to go, but we are put in the right. God maintains a lasting relationship with us. And this relationship lasts through eternity.

Romans 3:25–26 refers to the sacrificial act of Christ. In both the Old and New Testaments, the shedding of blood connotes the giving of life.[3] "For the life of the flesh is in the blood; and I have given it to you for making atonement for your lives on the altar; for, as life, it is the blood that makes atonement" (Lev. 17:11 NRSV). Christ has paid a price for our freedom. Read how Christ has the authority to guarantee it in Mark 1:27–28 and Matthew 7:28–29. Christ's life, death, and resurrection bring us into relationship and fellowship with God.

Questions for personal reflection

1. Explain this statement: "Sin, or missing the mark, causes us to fall short, but we do not fall from God's grace."

2. How does the free gift of grace show the true character of God?
3. Explain how the shedding of blood can take away sins (use Rom. 3:25–26 and Lev. 17:11 as references).
4. Concentrate on the last two important words of the paragraph on page 38: *relationship* and *fellowship*. What does a personal *relationship* with Christ mean? What sort of *fellowship* do you engage in? Do you seek Him each day? Do you give Him opportunity to speak through His Word as you read the Bible daily? Do you listen to Him as you pray?

Responsible for our pride

Paul was qualified to speak of boasting (3:27–28) because he struggled with pride. Pride and boasting exclude humility. Humility allows us to see ourselves as we really are, no better and no worse. As a young GA® in the 1960s, I remember studying the Beatitudes in Matthew 5. I was particularly impressed with "blessed are the meek" (v. 5). At the time, I was playing on a basketball team, and one of my teammates who was several years older seemed to embody this quality. Julie was quite good, but she never acted as though she felt she played better than the rest of us. Never taking credit for her exceptional play, she would instead praise the rest of the team. When Julie had an easy opportunity to score a basket, she often would opt to pass off to another team member and allow that person to score. At a young age, I was beginning to learn through Julie what meekness and humility were, but I often had difficulty practicing these. When I did succeed, I then wanted to take credit for my "righteousness" because I wanted to feel proud. This evil called pride is a deadly trait.

We do not need to glorify ourselves or disparage others in order to find favor in God's eyes. If we seek true humility, we may fail on two accounts: by not being truly humble, or by being humble and then being proud of it. The salvation we possess comes about in spite of ourselves and is therefore nothing to boast about.

Questions for personal reflection

1. Have you ever been proud of being humble? Explain.
2. Could it be that pride stands between you and God, preventing a perfect relationship? Decide now what you will do to get rid of your pride.

Responsible to proclaim to all nations

Romans 3:29–30 shows our obligation and call to proclaim the good news to all people. We can share the gracious gift of righteousness with everyone. We are not to keep it for ourselves, but we are to tell other thirsty pilgrims where to find water. The perpetual fountain is overflowing for all who are willing to partake.

Some Bible scholars think we can best understand the example of Abraham beginning with Romans 3:31. Read 3:31 through 4:9. Abraham was recognized as being righteous before God by faith, not by adherence to the law. He received justification before he was circumcised (4:10–11). Looking to our works instead of God's mercy fallaciously allows us to try to depend on ourselves. Thus we refuse to receive God's gift and generosity. We have not earned anything, but at times we want to be paid what we think we deserve (4:4), as did the laborers in Matthew 20:1–6 who turned up their noses at mercy.

One of my good friends keeps on her refrigerator a quote that her grandfather wrote decades ago. It says, "It's amazing the good that could be done in this world if no one were concerned with who got the credit." Who are we to say we deserve more than others? Who are we to think that we must be praised and rewarded for living as God would have us live?

Hope in God's great promise

If we could rely on what we earned, we would have no need of a promise. A religion of law would carry with it a dangerous pride if one could be successful in obeying the law (but that is impossible!). Legalism allows humans to put more stock in themselves instead of looking to God. While law makes us conscious of sin, with or without the law, we may accept God's promise by grace through faith.

One Christian educator named John Westerhoff has said that from the moment of birth we have faith. Why else do we cry?[4] While it's impossible to know that the cry of the infant shows faith that someone or something will offer help, no doubt at an early age we learn dependence and our faith is influenced by those early experiences. Built into that little bundle of joy is a mechanism that allows the young one to call out for care and nurture.

Early childhood influences may cause one to either gain or lose faith in caregivers. If the baby cries and her or his needs are met, the baby learns hope and gains confidence in the caregiver. If the baby repeatedly cries for assistance and no one comes to her or his aid, the baby gives up hope. Closely attached to hope is trust; and if hope is not established, the young one may have difficulty trusting parents and subsequently others in his or her life.

Some researchers in faith development believe that we project onto God the qualities that we see displayed in our parents. Fortunately my parents were wonderful providers and modeled godly behaviors that helped me to see God as nurturing and trustworthy. But all children are not so fortunate and many have difficulty learning trust. They have been betrayed too often and rejected too many times. Disappointment, abuse, and pain may have permeated their lives, and many of them wonder why God did not intervene. The faith of these wounded people may have been influenced negatively. Perhaps those of us who were fortunate enough to be well cared for have a gospel responsibility to those who were not.

Luke's words in 12:48 (NRSV) echo, "'From everyone to whom much has been given, much will be required.'" While God does not need us to teach trust and while we can never fully approach or model the characteristics of God, we can be present to those for whom trust has been defiled. How can we help those who have known little hope and trust in people to have faith in God?

Read Romans 4:13–16. Notice that God's original promise to Abraham of grace to all did not depend on the *law* but rather on the righteousness of *faith* (4:13). Because of Abraham's faith, God first stated the promise to him. The words *faith* and *trust* are often used synonymously. Martin Luther saw the two words as so similar that he used "the German word *vertrauen* (to trust) as a synonym for faith (*glauben*)."[5] From Abraham, the Redeemer came; hence, he is the father of faithfulness. Grace, not law, is operative here. God had to come up with a foolproof plan; and knowing the inevitable disobedience of human nature, God had to give us something we had no control over, something we could not rupture or defile. That "something" is God's wonderful grace.

Read verse 17. Notice that Isaac's birth was as though the dead had been made alive. Since Abraham and Sarah were both over 90 years old, Isaac was evidence that God can triumph in the midst of impossible odds (Gen. 17:17; 18:12). God can do whatever is necessary to ensure that the promise will be fulfilled. We can trust God to accomplish what we ourselves are impotent to do, and we are called to have hope in God's promises.

Obviously, faith was crucial to Abraham, and this faith, as Paul understood it, underlies the law and has priority over it (4:22). Faith does not annul the law but rather establishes it.[6] Faith bridges the chasm which separates us from God; and once that bridge has been crossed, we are expected to show evidence of our faith through our conduct.[7] This faith moves us to gospel responsibility.

The story of Abraham and Isaac troubled me as a young child and still does to an extent. Here we have in Genesis 22 a father obeying God by gathering up wood and taking his young son to the land of Moriah. I guess I identified with Isaac who wondered what in the world was going on. Now Isaac knew about sacrifices and even asked his father in verse 7 (NRSV), "'The fire and the wood are here, but where is the lamb for a burnt offering?'" I would have wondered the same thing and would have been extremely suspicious if my father had bound me up and placed me on top of a pile of wood as Abraham did in verse 9. Imagine what little Isaac must have felt. After hearing that story over and over as a child, I would often wonder how Isaac responded later when his daddy asked him to go on a little adventure with him, especially if they were carrying wood. I would not have been so sure about that trust issue. The story concerned me so much that I remember asking Mrs. Sharpe, my Sunday School teacher, if she thought that Sarah would have done that, if this mother would have set her son on fire if the ram had not appeared! These were tough questions for a little girl, and I must admit that I still ask some of the same questions. I sometimes wonder if the story is a good one for little children, and some educators say that maybe Bible stories such as this one might be better suited for older children. How do we respond when children, or adults for that matter, ask us difficult questions about faith and trust?

As Paul mentioned earlier, the law cannot ensure that humans will be obedient. The law cannot protect itself and is powerless in attempting to prevent sin. It can guarantee neither obedience nor salvation, but can simply serve as a guide. We as sinners will inevitably break the law. We must have something more promising to guarantee our eternity; that is the grace and mercy of God. Those people who are very advanced in faith development, according to James Fowler, do not need laws to provide boundaries for them. People like the late Mother Teresa are so moral and faithful that they would be obedient even if the law did not exist. Individuals at this stage of development are rare and possess a quality of selflessness that we seldom see. While these saintly faithful embody trust and love uncharacteristic of most of us, they are not perfect. Even though they have achieved a degree of faith that most of us will not approach, they are still fallible and in need of the grace of God.[8]

The most exciting news in this chapter is found in verses 23–25. Not Abraham alone, but all of us can be heirs to God's promises. Abraham's faith influences us to trust God with a vengeance. Having Jesus in our lives brings us a joy and a newness of life that moves us to love others and gives us a desire to share this unfathomable gift. This hope drives us toward gospel responsibility and gives us the opportunity to be faith influences in the lives of our neighbors.

Questions for personal reflection

1. Explain God's promise to Abraham (see Rom. 4:13).
2. How was Isaac a fulfillment of God's promise? How

did God teach Abraham to have faith despite the circumstances?
3. What do you think of Abraham's faithfulness? How do you think Isaac felt?

Accountable in peace and sacrifice

Read Romans 5:1–2 carefully. Being put right with God brings peace (5:1) which is more than an inner serenity and harmony. In John 14:27, Jesus contrasts the peace that He can give with the peace that the world gives. Like peace, faith (Rom. 5:1), hope (Rom. 5:4), and love (Rom. 5:5) are also available. Even in the midst of inevitable troubles, redemption overcomes the pain with a message of hope. Experiencing this crisis and adversity will cultivate patience and endurance.

Can you recall misbehaving and being taken out of church as a child, knowing the inevitable punishment that faced you on the other side of the door? At the age of about 2½, my cousin Jamison was fidgeting very badly in church one Sunday. My uncle John tried to reason with him, but Jamison was having trouble controlling himself. Finally his daddy had had enough of his shenanigans, picked Jamison up from the pew, and began walking toward the door. As they were about to step outside, little Jamison yelled back, "Somebody help me!"

All of us know how Jamison probably felt. Our punishment is no doubt deserved. But if we are repentant and we call out for help, we can be delivered from what is on the other side of the door!

Paul tells us that "while we were still sinners, Christ died for us" (5:8). Christ is kind to us, a friend in times of trouble, even when we are evil and ungrateful. In verses 9–11, notice what our source of joy is. Is it easier to feel responsible in times of joy or trouble?

We are accountable for our obedience to Christ. It is not easy to show accountability through sacrifice, but yielding to Him will bring peace and joy that only He can give. We may feel sinful, but we can turn to God even at our worst, and we are responsible to God to do just that. Maybe practicing that kind of responsibility can lead us to work in some of the ways Nakia mentioned at the beginning of this chapter. Maybe we can fill those handbaskets with hope and distribute it abundantly to those who could use a little optimism.

Questions for personal reflection

1. How are you accountable to serve God in peace?
2. Look at Paul's explanation of our growth during a crisis (vv. 3–5). What is the sequence of these verses? (____________ produces __________, which produces __________, which produces __________.) How have you experienced this in your own life?
3. How does redemption overcome pain with a message of hope? Do you recall a time when this happened to you?
4. How are you accountable to sacrifice for God?

[1]Clifton J. Allen, ed., *The Broadman Bible Commentary* (Nashville: Broadman Press, 1970), 10:182.
[2]George Arthur Buttrick, ed., *The Interpreter's Bible* (Nashville: Abingdon Press, 1978), 9:431.
[3]Ernest Best, *The Letter of Paul to the Romans* (London: Cambridge University Press, 1967), 43–44.
[4]John H. Westerhoff III, *Will Our Children Have Faith?* (Minneapolis: Seabury Press, 1976), 81.
[5]Douglas John Hall, *Thinking the Faith: Christian Theology in a North American Context* (Minneapolis: Augsburg, 1991), 249.

[6]Paul J. Achtemeier, *Romans*, vol. in *Interpretation: A Bible Commentary for Teaching and Preaching* (Louisville, KY: John Knox Press, 1985), 85.

[7]Buttrick, *Interpreter's Bible,* 9:441.

[8]James W. Fowler, *Faithful Change: The Personal and Public Challenges of Postmodern Life* (Nashville: Abingdon Press, 1996), 66–67.

4

Faith in God Brings Us Abundant Life

Romans 5:12 to 6:14

Our 12-year-old friend Nakia surprised her mother after the family's devotion on the sin of Adam. For months she and her family had been doing some serious Bible study. Her mother, a huge faith influence, had always encouraged her to think long and hard about what she read and to feel free to ask anything she wanted to about the Scriptures. Nakia's responses about Adam, Eve, the snake, and the apple were not the typical questions of a sixth-grader, but they certainly indicated that her theological wheels were turning. Perplexed by the blame she heard being placed on Adam, Nakia said, "I think Adam has gotten a bad reputation all these years for something anybody would have done." This precocious child further elaborated, "Why in the world did God stick that tree in the garden knowing that Eve would pick the fruit? And whoever started the rumor that it was an apple anyway?"[1]

Nakia's questions did not end here. Having read Genesis 3 during the family devotion she blatantly exclaimed, "For God to be so all-knowing, He certainly didn't seem to know what was going on in verses 8–13. Just look at all the questions He had to ask like, 'Where are you?'

and 'Who told you that you were naked?' and 'Have you eaten from the forbidden tree?' For Pete's sake, shouldn't an omniscient God have known the answers to those things?" She continued further, "I thought God knew everything and saw everything that we do. You would think that God would have had more of a clue about something that would affect the history of the world. And what if Adam and Eve had lied to God? Maybe we wouldn't have to work and maybe childbirth would be a breeze. And talk about holding a grudge! You mean it took all of those Old Testament years and all of the New Testament stuff up to Jesus being nailed on the Cross for God to say, 'OK, now I'll forgive that little snack in the garden.'"[2]

The questions of children often seem irreverent, too honest, and embarrassing, not to mention difficult. Some of these questions have a fairly simple explanation while others may be more controversial. How would you answer Nakia's questions if she were your child? More of Nakia's questions will follow in subsequent chapters, but first let's look at Adam and Christ.

Death and life—Adam and Christ—what a contrast when we look at these two figures in the Christian pilgrimage. In Romans 5:12 to 6:14, Paul addresses how Christians are accountable in life and how God's call brings us life in a world filled with sin and death. Throughout these passages, Paul shows several parallels between what Jesus and Adam experienced and what Christians may expect in light of these events.

Accountable in life

Read Romans 5:12–14*a*. For Paul, humanity connoted sinfulness. Humans perpetuate the sin of Adam. Paul fairly and accurately portrayed sin, neither minimizing its seriousness nor exaggerating its effects. It is a normal part of living in the world. We find it all around us every day. How then can we escape?

Many of the students and professors at the college where I teach come out of a fairly strict reformed tradition. When a question arises about why something bad has happened like the tragic death of a student or the Columbine High School massacre, the response is often, "Because we live in a fallen world." These people often point to the sin of Adam as the reason for these bad things happening to good people. Some people would say AIDS exists in order for God to purge the planet of homosexuals, and homosexuals exist because Adam ate the forbidden fruit. I ask my students what they think of these responses and I get mixed answers. Some say, yes, these tragedies are the result of the fallen nature of humans. But one said, "I don't understand what the bite of some fruit has to do with a truck crossing a median and hitting my friend's sports utility vehicle head on." Tragedies can often be linked to our sinfulness, but is "We live in a fallen world" always the appropriate answer and the only answer, particularly for individuals seeking reasons for their painful experiences?

If we continually point to the fall of humanity as the reason for evil, suffering, and death, how does this affect our outlook on life and the world? We too often hear the comment as Nakia pointed out previously, "The world is going to hell"; or "Society has gone to the dogs." People who have this outlook may throw up their hands when tragedy occurs and say, "Well, what do you expect in a fallen world?" Often we then excuse *ourselves* of responsibility here, not recognizing that *we* are the very individuals who make up society, and *we* just might be the ones who with God's aid can help the situation. Yes, humanity has sinned and sinned mightily, but we cannot continue to wallow in the notion that there is no hope.

Questions for personal reflection

1. Would you say Romans 5:12–21 is pessimistic and negative, or optimistic and positive?
2. Is all tragedy, death, and illness due to sin?

In the last chapter we looked at Paul's theme of universality or the idea that what we experience is universal to all people. Again in Romans chapters 5 and 6, Paul's theme of universality surfaces as he repeats what he expressed in Romans 3:23 (NRSV)—"All have sinned and fall short of the glory of God." However, Paul Achtemeier states quite succinctly, "Christ got us out of the mess Adam got us into."[3] Begin reading with Romans 5:14 (NRSV), "Adam, who is a type of the one who was to come."

Paul points out that just as Adam's act did tremendous harm to all, Christ's life and act can transform all who allow Him to. Read verse 15 (NRSV): "For if the many died through the one man's (Adam's) trespass." Do not be confused by the word *many* in this verse. This does not mean that some are exempt. *Many* actually means "all" here. Again, we can see how universal this verse is. While little Nakia would probably take issue with the idea that it was all Adam's fault, the verse applies to all of humanity.

Unity characterizes both the old race of Adam and the new race of Christ. All who call themselves Christian are united to achieve the goals Christ set. Spiritual poverty on the one hand and wealth on the other mark the sharp contrast between the old race shackled by sin and the new race freed by Christ.

Called to redemption and grace

The thrust of Paul's argument here is that grace triumphs over sin. The old hymn clearly states, "Grace that will pardon and cleanse within; . . . Grace that is greater than all our sin." Grace can reverse the effects of sin and death. That is, Christ's transforming power far outweighs any effects of Adam's transgressions, and to think that the two are equal shows a lack of understanding of the power of grace. Sin limits or restricts, but grace liberates and opens up our experience. Remember this: Evil is buried in a perpetual blizzard of grace.[4]

Since we inevitably will sin, we cannot depend on ourselves for redemption. Only God's free gift of grace is sufficient for that. Imagine a totally free gift available to all who will claim it, the sweepstakes of all sweepstakes. No return envelope or drawing is necessary. You possess the winning number, not due to your own effort but to God's mercy.

God does not ration this mercy. Instead, by faith, grace is available for the asking and everyone has the winning number. God does not place a price on it for several reasons. It has already been paid for; in addition, we could not afford it if it were for sale. Like oxygen, grace is both free and priceless, and without it, we will perish.

We don't need to be stingy and hoard the grace of God. Our disdain and anger toward people who disagree with us or hurt us often cause us to have feelings that we should closely examine. Some of us prefer grace and mercy for ourselves but justice and wrath for others. I once heard a man whose daughter had been killed by a drunk driver state, "I'll have a hard time enjoying heaven unless I can see that [person] rotting in hell." We say we want all the world to experience the joy in Christ that we have, when what we often really mean is they can have eternal life and be in heaven with me if they don't hurt me, if they believe exactly what I believe, if they're in the same denomination I'm in, if they have the same image of God I have, and if they vote the way I vote. If my student, Cassie, who was mentioned in chapter 1 had heard things like this all her life, no wonder she had grave reservations about associating with the Christians she knew.

Read verses 16–21. As you read, notice how this passage compares Adam's sin and death to Jesus' salvation and life. Perishing, or death, is the loss not just of biological life (the Greek *bios*) but also eternal life (usually *zoe* in the Greek).[5] While we all deserve this judgment or judicial sentence and condemnation, an "execution of the penalty,"[6] Christ intervenes and rescues us.

Imagine that you are about to receive a lethal injection, that you are strapped into the electric chair, or that you are seated in the gas chamber due to a crime that you have committed. If you have seen the films, *Dead Man Walking* or *The Green Mile,* this imagery will come easy to you. You sweat bullets as you pray that the governor will make the saving call to pardon your crime, but no such call comes. While you know without a doubt that you are guilty, you continue to hope and pray for mercy. At the last second, right before the executioner pushes the button or injects the fatal needle, the phone rings, the governor acquits you and allows you to go in peace. You can draw a parallel in your spiritual life. We know we are guilty of sin and deserve to be put to death for it, but Jesus steps in and acquits us. Paul says this acquittal does not merely guarantee physical life; it guarantees life eternal.

God's grace and Christ's power to pardon our sin are never-ending. Some Christians call this battle between sin and grace as "the 'war of the two queens,' since sin and grace are both feminine in Greek."[7] We are responsible and accountable for both sides of this battle. Again, that responsibility involves not just refraining from doing the bad but also includes seeking to do the good. It is our choice to sin, and it is our choice to allow grace through faith to triumph, to overcome death. We are accountable in life.

Questions for personal reflection

1. Which is worse, the loss of *bios* or *zoe*?
2. Make a list of comparisons in Romans 5:16–21. List Adam and all his traits on one side, and then list Christ and all His traits on the other side. How do the two compare?
3. How would you feel about that drunk driver enjoying heaven with you? How do you feel about that father's attitude toward the drunk driver who killed his daughter?

Called to newness of life

In Romans 6:1–9, Paul shows how Christians identify with Christ in several ways. Through baptism, we are united with Christ. Read verses 3–4. As Christ died for our deliverance, we die to sin. As Christ arose, God calls us to arise and walk in newness of life. Read verses 5–7. Christ breaks the grip of sin on us, transformed creatures. The new life in Christ demands that we no longer allow our bodies to be instruments of sin.

The fact that grace will abound in no way gives us license to continue to sin. Reread Romans 6:1–2,7. Paul knew that some would twist this idea of grace to suggest that we can facilitate God's gracious act by sinning as much as possible (read v. 15). However, when we identify with Christ, we have a new motive for doing good and being virtuous; we receive a new power and energy.

Baptism is the external sign for our acknowledgment. The three stages of baptism, "our descent into, our burial under, our rising from, the waters which symbolize regeneration," parallel the passion of Christ: crucifixion, burial, and resurrection.[8] We experience sacramentally what Christ experienced literally. Reread verses 4–6 to find these symbolic steps in baptism.

Being a water lover, the baptismal pool always intrigued me as a young child. Before I had ever seen an actual baptism, I was a bit afraid of what was behind that dark, scary curtain behind the choir loft. As young children do, I imagined all kinds of things that could be there. One of my favorite television shows at that time that had a tremendous faith influence on me was *Casper the Friendly Ghost.* Casper was such a good fellow and was always doing nice things for people, and I associated him a little bit with Jesus. All my life I had heard of the Holy Ghost and wondered if this might be Casper or at least like Casper. That was a comforting thought to me. So I got it into my head that maybe Casper the Holy Ghost lived behind that baptismal curtain.

Finally I got to see a baptism and began to figure this thing out. I understood what being a Christian meant, as much as a 9-year-old can, and wanted that for myself. For weeks I thought about trusting Jesus as my Lord and Savior and one Sunday night following Vacation Bible School commencement, I made a profession of faith in Christ. A few weeks later, it was time for my baptism.

Keep in mind that I was a water lover. All of us who were being baptized that night were told to bring a change of clothes since obviously the ones we were wearing would get wet. I was about in the middle of the line of children to be baptized, and I carefully watched as Dr. Jones, our interim pastor, dipped the children one by one into the water. Many of them came up crying, kicking, and sputtering with their white choir robes now nearly translucent. I thought, "They are such babies; they must not know how to swim."

When my time came I was so ready. Slowly I lowered myself into the water one step at a time until the water level was about up to my chin. Dr. Jones covered my nose with the white handkerchief that each of us had been told to bring and said, "I baptize you, my sister, in the name of the Father, the Son, and the Holy Ghost." (I couldn't help thinking a little bit about Casper at this point.) As Dr. Jones lowered me back in the water, its glorious warmth enveloped me. You see, I really loved being under water. When I emerged I heard him say something about rising to walk in newness of life. Dripping wet I climbed out of the pool, my clothes heavy with baptismal water. I had never been in the water with all of my clothes on, and it was almost as though the water were trying to suck me back in.

Finally out, I walked over and sat in the corner of the room where we were to change clothes. After a few minutes, Mrs. McCormick, one of the mothers helping us change, came over and said, "Tisa, you need to get on your dry clothes so that you can go out front and sit with the other children." I whispered to her shivering, "That's OK. I'm going to wait until everybody is dipped, and then I'm going to get back in and swim around for a little while if that's OK."[9]

That night when I got home I sat on the end of my bed and pondered the significance of this whole event. The "newness of life" phrase stuck in my brain, and I was determined to be different, to be better. Some days I was successful, and some days I wasn't, but the memory of that moment has lasted. Baptism meant something very important to me even as a 9-year-old.

Dale Moody says that being called to walk in newness of life is "a Hebrew way to express ethical conduct."[10] This walking requires voluntary effort on our part and suggests a beginning point, a quest, and a goal or destination. Unlike our warm, wet initial birth, which requires little effort on the part of the infant, newness of life, or rebirth, cannot occur without the consent and commitment of the Christian.

We do not ask to be born; we do ask to be *re*born. Pulling ourselves from that warm, comfortable water may be difficult, and often it would be nice to stay in there and swim around for a while. Sometimes it's cold out there, but the glow and warmth of Christ is there to lead us into newness of life.

Responsible to live with God through Christ

Read Romans 6:10–11 carefully in several translations. How does a Christian maintain the close fellowship with Christ mentioned in verse 8? My students often refer to their personal relationship with Christ. When I ask them what they mean by that, many of them give pretty insightful, well-thought-out answers. Others have a difficult time answering or else they give a pat answer that they have heard someone else say. Cognitively they know the right answer to give, but some of them do not *own* their responses. They have borrowed someone else's faith or the faith of the community of which they may have been a part for years. Wanting to belong, they go along with the consensus of the group. James Fowler calls this Synthetic-Conventional faith. This type of faith involves little critical reflection and little questioning.[11]

This kind of borrowed faith was exhibited in the responses to an exercise that I require of my class in a course on older adult development. Using someone over the age of 70, the students must conduct an interview then analyze and integrate the responses with what we have discussed during the semester. One of my students chose to interview Mrs. M., an 80-year-old woman who lived next door to the student's parents. Part of the interview centered on religious beliefs, and the woman who had been a Christian for 72 years gave a fairly standard answer to a question about her image of God. When asked how she knew that to be true, she responded, "Because that's what my father always told me." While this may be an appropriate response for a child who is young in the faith, is this a mature answer for someone who has known Jesus for more than seven decades? Little Nakia, mentioned in the first part of this chapter, had at age 12 already begun to critically examine her faith. But let me state clearly here that just because one person's style of faith differs from someone else's doesn't mean one has more faith than another. The difference is in the style of faith, not the degree of faith, in type, not quantity.

Becoming one with Christ suggests growth. As in John 15:1–8, we are grafted onto the vine of Christ. Taken further, this metaphor implies that attachment and commitment grow stronger and deeper as we mature in faith.[12] The graft "takes" and the vine does not reject it. This requires discipline on our part and means that we may need to give up some selfish aspects of our lives that interfere with our relationship with Christ. Our past must die along with the sin that enslaved us. I don't know about you, but sometimes my past rears its ugly head kicking and sputtering much like those children in the baptismal pool.

When a person dies with Christ, that person moves beyond the reach of evil. Death ends all claims on that person. We are no longer sentenced to life in prison once we have died; Paul says we are dead to sin (Rom. 6:11). Because Christ breaks this grip, we can now live under His lordship. Christ provides the guidelines and the nurture for this new life. We must provide the will and the discipline.

Questions for personal reflection

1. Explain what *death to sin* means in your own Christian experience.
2. How have you grown spiritually as a result of your Christian walk in newness of life?
3. What does spiritual growth look like to you? Is the type of faith you have now different from your childhood faith?

Responsible to yield God's grace

In Romans 6:12–14, Paul calls for an attitude change as well as a change in lifestyle. What we know to be true about God must relate to how we apply that truth to our own lives. Since sin is defeated, likewise our inner drives and appetites or what Freud calls the "id" must surrender. Theory and practice converge and we must take Jesus seriously. As we *know* the truth, God calls us to *do* the truth. Sin must not be our master, but God must become total Lord and Master of our lives. Reread verses 12–14 and decide if God is speaking to you about changes in one area of your life. Write down that problem area. Decide what you can do to indicate total surrender. God calls us to a righteous life and holds us responsible to live it, to get out of the baptismal pool and walk in newness of life.

Questions for personal reflection

1. In what way are you called to live out these verses? In what way are you responsible?
2. Why do you believe what you believe about newness of life?

[1]Tisa Lewis, "Spiritual Confessions of a Searching Boomer" (working title; unpublished manuscript), 65.
[2]Ibid., 66.
[3]Paul J. Achtemeier, *Romans*, vol. in *Interpretation: A Bible Commentary for Teaching and Preaching* (Louisville, KY: John Knox Press, 1985), 97.
[4]Ibid., 102.
[5]Clifton J. Allen, ed., *The Broadman Bible Commentary* (Nashville: Broadman Press, 1970), 10:195.
[6]Ibid., 196.
[7]Ibid., 197.
[8]George Arthur Buttrick, ed., *The Interpreter's Bible* (Nashville: Abingdon Press, 1978), 9:473.
[9]Lewis, "Spiritual Confessions of a Searching Boomer," 23.
[10]Allen, *Broadman Bible Commentary,* 10:199.
[11]James W. Fowler, *Faithful Change: The Personal and Public Challenges of Postmodern Life* (Nashville: Abingdon Press, 1996), 61–62.
[12]Buttrick, *Interpreter's Bible,* 9:475.

5

God's Call Frees Us

Romans 6:15 to 7:25

Slavery and *bondage* are difficult words for many Americans to understand, especially white Americans. The television miniseries, *Roots*, which aired many years ago gave some Americans the first graphic glimpse of slavery that they had ever seen. While some of our ancestors may have been slaves or owned slaves, the concept is far removed from twenty-first-century America. Or is it?

Responsible to the master

Little Nakia, the precocious child we met previously, was trying to figure out the references to slavery in the New Testament. Nothing got by her, and as we've seen before, she wasn't shy about asking anything that confounded her. Being African American, she had heard stories about her ancestors who were bought and sold as property, so this talk of slavery had a special meaning for her that I as a white woman cannot begin to understand. Let's look at what Paul has to say about slavery and bondage in both Romans and Ephesians and then listen to Nakia's questions about these passages.

Slavery and obedience go hand in hand. Paul knew his readers could identify with the slavery image since many of them were slaves.[1] Read Romans 6:15–17. You may want to compare several translations. Notice the two kinds of slavery: slavery to sin or slavery to righteousness. Now, read Ephesians 6:5–6. Slaves were to obey their human masters but were also to be slaves of Christ. Paul says clearly that we are slaves to whatever we obey; so modern Americans can easily understand this image since we are all obedient to something or somebody.

The slavery image in Romans 6:15–17 refers to our moral allegiance. Two masters cannot own the same slave. If one master claims ownership, his or her slave is not obligated to anyone else. Essentially, being subject to one master frees us from any other responsibilities. If we are slaves to righteousness, we are free from exercising sin. However, the converse is also true. We must choose whom to serve.

This would be comparable to a soldier trying to obey orders from two different commanding officers or one employee trying to work for two bosses. Take the example of a violinist in an orchestra with two conductors. Imagine the chaos and frustration that she and the other musicians would experience as they tried to follow one conductor who wanted to increase the tempo and the other who wanted to slow things down. The music this orchestra produced would not be something I'd want to pay to hear.

Slavery seemed like a scary thing to Nakia. She could not understand how something so bad and unethical could have been acceptable to Paul, even to the point of his telling slaves to actually obey their masters. Nakia said, "I'll bet slave owners got a lot of mileage out of that Ephesians passage that told slaves to obey them 'with fear and trembling'" (Eph. 6:5 NRSV). She continued, "Why did Paul say those things? Didn't he know that this could not be right? And when did folks finally get a clue that maybe this slave thing was not something God wanted? I wonder what other things that Paul wrote about might make God shake His head."

No doubt the issue of slavery has raised questions even to the point of people dying over their convictions about the issue. But the point of the passage is that we cannot waffle between obedience to one Lord and allegiance to a competing master. The choice is often difficult, and each of us is free to choose whom we will serve.

Questions for personal reflection

1. Spend a few moments imagining you are a slave. How would your life change? How would serving an earthly master differ from serving the heavenly Master? Which would be more difficult?
2. How would you respond to Nakia's comments and questions?
3. What master other than Christ sometimes commands your allegiance?

Accountable to be servants and to bear fruit

Once we choose whom our master is, life becomes less complicated. When we encounter a situation, we do not need to stop and consider on which side we will stand. As Paul Achtemeier says, "Paul is clear. 'The devil made me do it' will no longer work as an excuse."[2] When the Flip Wilson character said, "The devil made me do it," we laughed and saw that sketch as entertainment. However, many of us still use that excuse and see evil personified. Again we might say, "I just can't control those evil impulses that come over me." Unfortunately human nature is often next to impossible to tame, and all of us struggle with selfish urges. If we opt for sin, we fall more deeply into it. However, if we opt for righteousness, we will grow more strongly toward Christ. In Romans 6:18 (NRSV), Paul says once we are set free of sin we become "slaves of righteousness."

You may have heard the illustration of the frog in hot water. I wouldn't try this, but I've heard it's true. If you throw a frog in very hot water, it will immediately jump out. But if you put the same frog in a pot of water at room temperature and slowly turn up the flame under the pot, the frog will adjust to the rising heat until it is boiled alive. Small sins, if such things exist, often get hold of us and we commit them over and over to the point that we don't even notice them. Gradually our tolerance for sin may increase to the point that we need more and more of a stimulus to satisfy us. The next thing we know we are hooked into something that is over our heads and often beyond our escape.

Slavery to sin offers little except a cumulative effect: the more we sin, the more our better qualities deteriorate. Like a malignant tumor that metastasizes, sin spreads and infiltrates every fiber of our beings, and even the healthy areas are eventually affected. As Paul states in Romans 6:19, greater and greater iniquity results in our being progressively cut off from God. "For the wages of sin is death, but the free gift of God is eternal life in Christ Jesus our Lord" (v. 23 NRSV).

Here "wages" implies doing one thing to get something else we deserve. This involves an active component and expenditure of time and effort. However, a free gift in no way connotes reward for work, but is undeserved. In the Christian life, we must accept the free gift of salvation because of God's grace. The two poles of *wage* and *grace* contrast strikingly.

As you might guess, Nakia, now 14 years old, raises her hand again here. More confused about "free gift" than she is "wages" she asks, "Does *free* mean 'free' or are there strings attached? How does the sheep and goats story (Matt. 25) figure in here? My Bible says in red that Jesus said we would go into eternal fire (v. 41) if we didn't feed the hungry, clothe the naked, and visit the prisoners. That doesn't sound like a 'free gift' to me."

How do you interpret "free gift" here? Is this where gospel responsibility comes in again? How does grace fit into this story from Matthew?

Becoming a slave of righteousness requires that those who are strong in the faith nurture those who are newly set free from sin's bondage. In much the same way that a parole officer watches out for one who has been released from prison, those who profess a new allegiance to Christ require caring attention. Daniel Aleshire has even coined a word for this: *faithcare.*[3]

The situation is similar to a school graduation. Graduates feel like birds let out of a cage. No longer are they tied down with exams, papers, and demanding professors; but they enter a new regime. The graduates must then consider new responsibilities even though they experience freedom. They still must be obedient to the rules and norms of society. All of that credit card debt that they accumulated while buying books, computers, software, clothes, and CDs must be paid off. When the rent is due, when the roof begins to leak, and when the pressures of a 9:00-to-5:00 job bear down, new graduates may long for the predictability of the cafeteria and the classroom and the safety of the dormitory. However, they must face new responsibilities, and the Christian must surrender to a new lordship. Those who are stronger in the faith can provide support and encouragement to new Christians.

Questions for personal reflection

1. Contemplate the principle in verse 18. Which comes first, being set free, or being servants of righteousness?
2. Use Romans 6:19 as a "before-and-after" exercise. List words associated with *before Christ* and then list those associated with *after.*
3. In what ways can you support and encourage new Christians?

Responsible under the law

Paul's letter uses the marriage illustration to point out that death ends all legal obligations. Note the illustration Paul gives in Romans 7:1–6. Hebrew law dictated that a woman was her husband's personal possession.[4] As Paul stated in 1 Corinthians 7:39, a woman was free to marry someone else if her husband died and only if he died. That is, death dismissed any legal obligation that the woman had.[5] When we die to sin, we can be united to Christ, Who takes the role of the pure, legal second husband.

The choice of analogy and words that Paul uses here is interesting. We learn something about marriage in Paul's day when he presents this analogy. Some would say the phrases "bound by the law" (v. 2); "free from that law" (v.3); and "held us captive" (v. 6) shed a less than positive light on the marriage enterprise. Beverly Gaventa in the *Women's Bible Commentary* points out that the wife is understood as a function of her husband and his longevity.[6] Is she to an extent held captive as his slave? At what point in history did this cease to be the case? Why is the husband not held to the same level of commitment as the wife? The correlation of the idea of Christ becoming the pure, legal second husband and the advice in

Ephesians 5:25 for husbands to love their wives as Christ loved the church illuminates the gospel responsibility of husbands to their wives. Being loved as Christ loved the church is a far cry from being held captive as a slave. What a contrast; but these two extremes in marriage might still be operative in the twenty-first century.

While at times individuals try to maintain their relationship to God through legalism, Christ dismissed the necessity of that by freeing us from legalism's bondage. The law is imperfect, but Christ's perfection abounds. Christ is now in us and the law becomes secondary. How wonderful it is to know that we can be united with perfection.

Paul also uses the image of marriage to reinforce the level of intimacy available through a relationship with the perfect Christ. This marriage should then bear fruit. As Ernest Best states, "The activities of the new life of righteousness when the believer is married to Jesus will be like the children of a marriage."[7] Just as children are the fruit of a marriage, good works are the fruit of our relationship with Christ. While the law no longer enslaves us, our actions (fruits) do matter.[8] The analogy, however, breaks down when we consider that the term *barren* is seldom used today to describe a woman who is childless. Being childless in our culture today is much more acceptable than it was in previous centuries. However, if our spiritual lives are barren, this is unacceptable to God. Our motivation toward righteousness, however, should not come from the external compulsion to follow rules. Christians cannot legislate morality. Instead, our motivation must be intrinsic and come from the indwelling of God's Spirit (v. 6). God's spirit directs our morality.

Questions for personal reflection

1. According to Romans 7:2, what were the conditions under which a woman's marriage was dissolved? Why do you think the same did not hold true for the husband?
2. What would cause a woman to be labeled as an adulteress (see v. 3)? Why did this law change? Did the change in the law connote a weakening of the marriage bond or a cultural difference between today and Paul's day?

Accountable and delivered from the law

Read Romans 7:7–12. The law will bring to light our sense of sin. Paul says, "What then should we say? That the law is sin? By no means! Yet, if it had not been for the law, I would not have known sin. I would not have known what it is to covet if the law had not said, 'You shall not covet'" (v. 7 NRSV). Paul explains how the law shows us right from wrong and reflects our sin like a mirror to show us how sinful we have been. When we are told we cannot have something, we want it even more than before. Being forbidden to eat chocolate or popcorn will sometimes make you crave it, eat it, and then feel guilty about it. Breaking a forbidden law often results in guilt. However, it is not the forbidding law but the reality of God that will help us move from our mediocre ways of life to a vibrant life under divine authority. The nudging of the Holy Spirit urges us to repent, and God washes away the guilt as we are redeemed.

Our little friend Nakia found this passage a bit difficult to understand. "You mean Paul is saying that if the Ten Commandments had not been written, I could steal a CD from Wal-Mart and think that was OK, that I wouldn't know 'stealing' was something bad?" She continues, "And if I shoot my teacher, you mean I would see that as an acceptable thing to do? Don't you think that most people's conscience would work even if we didn't have the laws?"

Nakia raises some interesting questions about conscience. Is conscience something we are born with, or do life experiences, even laws, cause conscience to be formed and developed? What causes some people to have stronger consciences than others? Do they have more faith influences in their lives to guide them? Or is conscience the dwelling of the Holy Spirit within us? Part of our conscience may be the function of something called EQ, or emotional intelligence, that we will discuss later.

You have often heard the phrase, "Well, she just didn't know any better." But this excuse is not always valid and doesn't always work. One moonlit summer night I was driving down Highway 9 on my way to North Myrtle Beach in South Carolina. Most of the time I'm pretty good about watching the speed limit signs, but I had not seen one for miles after I pulled out of a gas station. Having been used to a speed limit of 65 MPH on similar roads in North Carolina, I assumed the limit was the same on this stretch of highway. My assumption was dead wrong. Maybe you have had that sick feeling when you see a blue light in your rearview mirror. Well, I had been caught. The polite officer asked if I had any idea how fast I was driving, and I responded, "Sixty-eight." You see, my cruise control was set so I knew exactly how fast I was going, and I figured about 3 miles over the limit would be acceptable. (Most of us push our limits here and have our own opinions on what this figure really is.) "The speed limit is 55 MPH here," said Officer Friendly. (That really was his name!) I responded truthfully, "Oh! I had no idea. I thought it was 65 MPH." This excuse did not work, and I ended up supporting the state of South Carolina's highways with my money order for $50. I was still responsible even though I did not know that particular law. Obviously speeding is not in the same category as the Ten Commandments, but often we are responsible even when "we don't know any better."

Doing something illegal like speeding is not always considered sinful. Interestingly enough, many things that are sinful are often not illegal. Take the example of hoarding money and not sharing it with those in need. As long as we pay our taxes, we can hoard all the money we want. Maybe it's sinful, but it's not illegal.

Many things in Paul's day that are now illegal and in my opinion, sinful, were acceptable and not considered unlawful. We've already mentioned slavery and treatment of women as property. Other examples include concubinage and very early marriage for girls as young as 11 or 12. In the Old Testament, parents were even encouraged to have their rebellious sons stoned to death by the elders of the town (Deut. 21:18-21). While this would certainly curtail juvenile delinquency, we see this today as being quite extreme. We see this, along with the other examples above, as even deplorable. Likewise, some things that were considered sinful and/or illegal in Paul's day are now considered by most people to be acceptable, such as the previously mentioned adultery of the woman who remarried before her first husband was dead. We often need to reexamine our definition of sin.

In Romans 7:11, Paul explains that sin is an opportunist. Here again, we see sin personified as if it has a mind of its own. Like a virus or a bacterium, it can catch us at our most vulnerable moments when our defenses are down, weaken us further, and then move in for the kill. Sin does not relent until we are totally defeated. However, *sin* and *law* must not be confused. The law is holy and merely exposes sin. It does not make us sin any more than the physician who diagnoses our illness makes us sick.[9] The law merely sheds light on what is happening. Paul makes it clear that we cannot blame the law for our sinfulness. In Romans 7:12 (NRSV) he writes, "So the law is holy, and the commandment is holy and just and good."

Questions for personal reflection

1. How did Paul know lust was wrong?.
2. Elaborate on Romans 7:11. How has sin deceived you and "killed" you in your personal life?
3. In addition to the example of committing adultery by marrying before the first husband is dead, are other things condemned by Paul now considered acceptable or not sinful?
4. Explain this sentence: "Sin is an opportunist."

Faith influences inner conflict

Willing and *doing* are continually in conflict. Again in Romans 7:13–25, as in Romans 6:23, Paul contrasts two poles here, the spiritual and the mortal, or physical. Like Paul, you may know what you should do and you may even want to do it, but the flesh is weak. Your intentions are good, but the problem comes when you try to carry out those good intentions and continually fail. Here Paul's words are in the form of a letter and are not intended as official doctrine, but he had quite a bit of insight into human nature as he wrote to his friends in Rome.[10] Look carefully at verse 15. Have you ever experienced this dilemma? Have you ever done the very thing you were trying to avoid? Have you ever slipped up and done something you hated, perhaps being guilty of some behavior you despised in others? It's almost as though an evil self is battling with a decent self trying to gain control over our beings. Our human condition brings frustration.

One of my students, Denise, confided in me that she had struggled with bulimia for several years. Bulimia is a frustrating eating disorder that affects many college students, particularly females. The bulimic individual gets totally out of control when it comes to eating, often binging on foods that are high in carbohydrates and then purging by vomiting or by using laxatives and diuretics.

Denise was constantly burdened with the guilt that she felt when she binged and purged, which was often. Not only was guilt of being a glutton a problem, but she was also beginning to suffer other physical effects from her disease. For years Denise's parents and pastor told her that all she needed was to ask God to deliver her from this sin and have faith that God was in control.

Denise was a strong Christian and took to heart what her spiritual leaders had told her. When she came to me, not only did she have the guilt over her bulimia, she also had even more guilt that her faith was not strong enough to heal her, that she was not a good enough Christian. What would you have done if this young woman had come to you with this problem? She knew what she needed to do but felt too weak to overcome her problem, much the way Paul felt in verses 15–19. Still relying on God's help, after much prayer and a little research, Denise entered a treatment program that helped her get her eating disorder under control.

Paul's frustration was apparent as he recognized he was helpless and in need of God's aid. He knew that he was not alone in his struggle but that Christ could offer him incredible strength and power. Christ offers us that same kind of strength today. While Paul's own strength and power were defeated, he was elated and cried out in gratitude to God for delivering him from the depths of despair. It is comforting to know that God can deliver us from despair as completely as He delivered Paul from it.

We should not make the mistake of believing that a behavioral disorder or a chemical imbalance causes all sin in our lives. But neither should we make the mistake of avoiding treatment for behavioral problems and disorders by saying we will just wait for God to intervene. Often God may be telling us to get help. In Denise's case, prayer certainly helped her feelings of despair, and she felt that part of God's answer to her was to seek professional treatment.

Questions for personal reflection

1. Explain Romans 7:15 in your own words. Give an example of how this happened to you.
2. How do spiritual and physical factors work against each other in your life? How can they work together?
3. Can we be too dependent on God to deliver us from temptations that result in destructive behaviors? Do we sometimes need professional help to move from prayer to action?

Called to God's purposes

Perhaps the words that best sum up much of what Paul is saying to us in these passages can be found in the hymn:

> Softly and tenderly Jesus is calling,
> Calling for you and for me;
> See on the portals He's waiting and watching,
> Watching for you and for me.
> Come home, come home,
> Ye who are weary come home;

Earnestly, tenderly Jesus is calling,
Calling, O sinner, come home.

Paul continued expressing his thanksgiving to God for the soft and tender call of Christ in his second letter to Timothy. Read 2 Timothy 1:1–9. We, like Timothy, can shoulder the suffering that will come in telling the good news as God gives us strength. "He saved us and called us to be his own people" (2 Tim. 1:9), not by our merit but by the free gift of grace. Like the slaves mentioned at the beginning of this chapter, we can be freed by the love of Christ. Thanks be to God for freeing us.

[1]Clifton J. Allen, ed., *The Broadman Bible Commentary* (Nashville: Broadman Press, 1970), 10:202.
[2]Paul J. Achtemeier, *Romans*, vol. in *Interpretation: A Bible Commentary for Teaching and Preaching* (Louisville, KY: John Knox Press, 1985), 109.
[3]For a description of this kind of caring attention, see Daniel O. Aleshire, *Faithcare: Ministering to All God's People Through the Ages of Life* (Philadelphia: Westminster Press, 1988).
[4]Allen, *Broadman Bible Commentary,* 10:205.
[5]Ibid.
[6]Beverly Roberts Gaventa, "Romans," in *The Women's Bible Commentary*, ed. Carol A. Newsom and Sharon H. Ringe (Louisville, KY: Westminster/John Knox Press, 1992), 318.
[7]Ernest Best, *The Letter of Paul to the Romans* (London: Cambridge University Press, 1967), 78.
[8]Ibid.
[9]Allen, *Broadman Bible Commentary,* 10:209.
[10]George Arthur Buttrick, ed., *The Interpreter's Bible* (Nashville: Abingdon Press, 1978), 9:501.

6

Gospel Responsibility Is a Walk in the Spirit

Romans 8:1–39

Do you ever feel like you have an evil twin inside you talking you into doing things that the good twin knows are wrong?" asked Nakia. In the previous chapter we looked at the nature of sin and our human weakness in trying to overcome the urges to do evil. This chapter continues to explore the frustration we often feel when our flesh calls us in one direction and the spirit of God calls us in another. Using the idea of the family of God, we will examine our responsibility to be good sons and daughters. Little Nakia makes another appearance as she helps us explore in an apocryphal way what Jesus' family might have looked liked. All of this may move us to a better understanding of how these many faith influences help transform us to be agents of gospel responsibility.

The battle between human nature and God's Spirit rages constantly. In chapter 8 of Paul's letter to the Romans, he affirms that God's Spirit accomplishes what the law could not. This battle between human nature and God's Spirit is a one-sided contest because the Spirit is by far the more powerful. In this chapter, Paul gives us one of the most optimistic messages revealed in the Scriptures.

Responsible and spiritually minded

Read carefully Romans 8:1–11. Look at how many times Paul uses the word *flesh* in these verses (NRSV). The Bible constantly refers to the flesh as weakness but not necessarily sin. We might substitute the words *human nature* for *the flesh*. Human nature reflects an attitude, and this attitude becomes sinful when it is destructive. The two contrasts in this passage (vv. 1–11)—*Spirit* and *the flesh*—illustrate two ways of living. Think of life as a drama. One question might be, Is the script already written or do we write it as we go? How much leeway do we have in interpreting the intent or purpose of the story? Once the script is written, can it be changed or are we stuck with the first draft? We do have a choice in the way the drama is played out. Living a life controlled by the flesh often leaves God backstage or in the wings. We can live in rebellion and idolatry or in a new order of freedom and joy made possible by the Spirit. The choice then is whether to self-direct or to allow God to be the director in this drama.

Look at Romans 8:9–11. When we live in the Spirit, Christ dwells in us. The motives for everything we do will stem from an understanding and a willingness to be like Christ. We will inevitably sin, but Christ has taken care of our weakness. In her book, *Educating in Faith: Maps and Visions,* Mary Boys uses the analogy of cartography, or the art of mapmaking, to help us understand what it means to educate in faith with a desired journey.[1] Living by the Spirit helps us map out a plan with a purpose.

Obviously the destination we choose is crucial, but the quality of the trip is also important. After the course has been charted, we may take detours and wrong turns. But the Compass will get us back on track and continue to point us toward our goal. No doubt we will constantly have to stop and ask for directions, and the Spirit is there to guide us to our destination. Many of our routes will be long stretches that are plain and ordinary, but sometimes the journey is exciting and scenic. Along the way we will encounter numerous faith influences and will daily have opportunities to stop along the way and influence the faith of others, to help them make their own maps. As we go we can be assured that Christ is a reliable Compass, and we can be certain that He will not lead us astray.

Some of the roads we choose will be nicely paved with new asphalt, and others will be rough dirt paths with washed out gullies. When we make a wrong turn, sometimes a road will lead to a dead end, and we'll have to backtrack to get onto a thoroughfare. If we are preoccupied and get off the beaten path, all kinds of snares are there to interrupt our journey or maybe as we will see in 8:28, to teach us something. But these preoccupations with things that are not of God, these selfish excursions will enslave, spoil, and defile us. Consider these truths: (1) our interests will dictate what our personalities will be; and (2) we will become what we think.

Nakia was troubled by her inability to be good. She had wonderful intentions but could not always carry through with them. When her brother Michael aggravated her, she would lash out at him. Once when he bothered her as she washed dishes, she threw a fork at him that stuck in his rear. At other times when Michael was minding his own business, she would taunt him just to get on his nerves.

At age 14, Nakia's thoughts began to turn to boys, and she had to admit that some of her thoughts were not exactly godly. Beginning to get quite a bit of attention from the boys in her class, she made a decision that Friday night at Tasha's birthday party, she would kiss Rodney Johnson for the first time. Rodney had had his eye on Nakia for some time, so her advances toward him were quite welcomed.

The party was a great success, if you know what I mean, and Nakia could not get Rodney off of her mind. Her first kiss was everything she had imagined. It was also some things she had never imagined. Thoughts of Rodney invaded her dreams, and sometimes she was quite embarrassed when she awakened. "Where does some of that stuff come from?" she asked her mother to whom she always told everything. "Thoughts just seem to pop into my head sometimes, pretty much beyond my control. I don't understand how I think some of the things that I think. My mind seems to have, you know, a mind of its own or something."

Nakia genuinely wanted to set her mind on pure thoughts and believed that if she focused more on her relationship to Jesus, those thoughts would disappear. She never watched TV shows or movies that would, in her words, "be a bad influence." But hard as she tried, crazy ideas would still sometimes occur over which she seemed to have little control. Worried about her spiritual well-being, Nakia asked her mother if this was normal and what she should do about it. She said, "How do I make the God thoughts outweigh the other thoughts?"

As a student of biology, psychology, and theology, I have always been intrigued by how the human body, mind, and spirit work together. In our rapidly changing world science and technology are allowing us to discover things that during my childhood could not even be imagined. Recent findings tell us that certain areas of the brain are responsible for how, how often, and to what extent we think about God. You may have seen TV reports on health and faith in 1999 that highlighted these findings. One area of the brain in the temporal lobe seems to house the capacity for us to think about God and have spiritual and religious experiences. What's even more interesting is that part of the body's immune system that helps us ward off disease and fight infection is housed in this same area of the brain. Some researchers then wonder if this is the reason why people who have strong faith live longer and are often better able to recover from health problems. This area in the temporal lobe may also control how intensely a person responds to the religious experiences that he or she has. In all of this, researchers are quick to stress that "these findings do not negate the validity of God, but merely suggest that humans may be 'hard wired' for . . . divine communication."[2]

How does a thought occur, and how much control do we have over the things that pop into our heads? The Spirit may certainly induce the holy thoughts that we have. Surely some of our thoughts come about because of things we have observed or experienced either directly or vicariously. But haven't you ever had a dream where the material was so outlandish or so depraved that you could not imagine how it surfaced? Fortunately we do have control over whether we act on those thoughts, and some people seem to have more control than others.

Nakia's thoughts were pretty mild compared to some of the thoughts that come to mind for some people. Explanations of thought and behavior are not excuses for evil actions, but sometimes these explanations help us avoid future problems. Let's look at a much more disturbing example. Tony was a 47-year-old father of two who struggled with the urge to rape. He could be lying in bed with his wife and an urge so powerful would come over him that he would leave his wife in bed to go out and find his next victim. Month after month, year after year he violated women, most of whom he had never even met. Each time after these horrendous acts, he would pray to God to deliver him from the evil that caused him to sin so horribly. Finally, after he had raped his 23rd victim, he was apprehended and is now serving a life jail sentence. Let me state up front that Tony has confessed his unspeakable crimes and believes he should be punished for life. As a matter of fact, he says he would understand perfectly if the state chose to execute him. When he was put in jail, he was on suicide watch because of an attempt to kill himself the first night. His actions were totally unacceptable not just to society but also to himself. Blood tests showed that he had a testosterone level that was more than four times normal.

A relative of mine was raped, and I have no sympathy for rapists. This is a violation of women that is said by some to be worse than death. In no way do I believe that an elevated testosterone level justifies the kind of behavior that we see in Tony or any other criminal. Before we had had a chance for discussion, one of my students got irate when I used this case study in one of my classes. This student told me that I was trying to medicalize sin. But some of these students who will be working in the prison system will be dealing with men like Tony and need to figure out how to handle these prisoners with drugs like Depo-Provera which reduces the urge to attack once they are incarcerated. My students asked me if I believe hormones and chemicals can contribute to sinful behavior. As one who deals with low blood sugar myself, I know that around 5:00 P.M. I sometimes get so cranky and out of sorts that I scare myself. My childhood friend Carol's husband is considering leaving her because he cannot handle her rage. Carol, who suffers from clinical depression, admits that at times this rage is so overwhelming that she gets completely out of control. Like Nakia she asks, "Where does this come from, and why do I act this way?" But, again, no level of blood sugar or any other chemical is an excuse to sin. Not all rapists have elevated testosterone levels, and, as mentioned in the last chapter, not all sins are rooted in our biological makeup. As one of my students would say, "Some people are just plain mean." However, it is important to understand the reasons why we sometimes behave the way we do and also to realize that biology is not destiny.

The good news here is that while the flesh is weak, God's Spirit gives us the promise of new life. Read carefully the promises that God gives us in Romans 8:10–11. Flesh and bones—the Spirit's ability to recreate a new people is similar to Ezekiel's reference to dry bones in Ezekiel 37:1–14. Essentially, we are called back from the dead.[3] No longer should we dwell on our sinful pasts or the wrongs we have committed. We are responsible to let go of all that and not resist what the Spirit can do. Orthodoxy or right belief alone is not enough. We must possess the Spirit of Christ. If our lives do not reflect that Spirit, claiming to be a Christian is pointless.

Questions for personal reflection

1. How do you contrast living by the flesh with living by the Spirit in your own life? Divide a sheet of paper into two columns. On one side, list acts directed by the flesh; on the other side, list acts directed by the Spirit.
2. How would you answer the question about bad thoughts that Nakia asked her mother? Are those thoughts normal? Are they controllable?
3. Give examples of this truth: You will become what you think. How can you change your thought processes?
4. Do you exhibit any behaviors over which you feel you have little control? How do you handle this? How are Paul's words helpful here?

Responsible to be the sons and daughters of God

You probably know how it feels to be treated like family. Being a member of a family carries with it certain privileges.

We do not have to put up fronts or fear being rejected. Being a family member also carries responsibility and connotes unity.[4] Caring, sharing, and "just being there" for each other promotes good family relations. Selfishness, disregard for others, and wanting one's own way can kill a family.

Notice that Romans 8:12–17 describes the ideal family. Nakia expressed her disappointment to her mother that the Bible gives us little information about Jesus' biological family. She said, "So much of the New Testament is about Jesus' birth, death, and resurrection. That's good, but what about the 18 or so years from the time He got yelled at for getting left behind in the temple (Luke 2:41–52) and the time He was 30-something. I wish we knew what Jesus was like as a little boy and more about His family."

Nakia then lets her imagination run wild. She begins, "Imagine I am Jesus' niece. The Son of God is my mother's brother, rather, half-brother, and His mother Mary is my grandmother. Just think; my mother's older brother is the most famous person to ever walk on the planet! At family reunions we always want Uncle Jesus to be there to say the blessing and in case we run out of food. I try to be like Him, following Him around, sometimes trying on His big old dusty sandals. Occasionally I ask Him, 'Uncle Jesus, would you do a miracle for me, just a little one?' The story that I hear all the time at family reunions is when Uncle Jesus was a little boy, one day he ran out of the house to play and forgot to shut the door. Great-aunt Martha who had a problem with long-term memory yelled, 'Jesus, were You born in a barn?!'"

Digressing even further, Nakia asks, "Did Uncle Jesus' grandmother bake cookies for Him? After all, He was the first grandchild. Did His uncle take Him fishing? Did His aunt, the one who yelled at Him, pinch His cheek and say, 'My, Jesus, how you have grown!" Did his grandfather give Him a hammer for His birthday, or would that be Christmas? When Uncle Jesus was 8 or 9, did Mary pull Him on her lap and tell Him about the night He was born and remind Him that she used to change His diapers? Just imagine if Jesus had been my uncle and my Savior! "[5]

Wouldn't it be nice if we did know more about Jesus' early life and family? The Gospel of Thomas which obviously was not included in the canon does give us some delightful stories of Jesus as a little boy that some would say seem a bit far-fetched. But these stories do spur our imagination and make us wonder about His whole life. The family dynamics of the Son of God could certainly shed some light on how to be a sibling and a son or daughter. Paul tells us in the following passage how we are all children of God in one big family.

Count how many times in Romans 8:12–17, Paul mentions a family word, like *brother*, *son*, or *children*. We are included in that family relationship as growing Christians. Being adopted by God should mean that we now think differently about God. While nothing is required of us to be adopted initially, a good daughter or son reciprocates the love of his or her parents, the way I'm sure Jesus did. Here God's *will* for us takes on two different meanings. The estate has been settled, the will has been read, and we are beneficiaries in an incredible way. As we receive a payoff, an inheritance, we will share as heirs of God's love and power exhibited in the birth, life, death, and resurrection of Christ.

Turn to Romans 8:18. Part of the responsibility of being in God's family involves taking on the role of a fellow sufferer with Christ. Now read verses 19–23. Humans often duplicate the experience of nature. If you have given birth to a child you can certainly understand the vivid analogy that Paul uses. In this passage, Beverly Gaventa points to the maternal role of ushering in a new age.[6] As the expectant mother groans in anticipation of the birth of her new creation, we do the same as we look forward to our adoption with hope. Paul says our present suffering is nothing compared to the benefit we will receive.

Not only do we suffer, but our earth suffers as well. Nature is affected as we both knowingly and unknowingly exploit and pollute our environment. However, we should not despair and take on a fatalistic attitude. God gives us minds to examine the damage to our environment that we have caused and helps us figure out how to correct or at least reduce future damage. We should take responsibility for the waste and pollution, examine global warming, and take steps to protect the world with which God has so abundantly blessed us. Hopeful attitudes affect optimistic anticipation, and that anticipation leads to enthusiastic action.

Read Romans 8:24–25. How many times does Paul mention *hope*? We can have hope because God gives it plentifully. The hope God gives helps us endure suffering with patience. It encourages us to anticipate optimistically and to act responsibly and realistically.

As we moved into a new century, quite a bit of focus was on the stock market, particularly technology stock. Like picking a horse at the Kentucky Derby, people were trying to guess which stock would have the highest gains, especially with so much focus on computer systems, wireless communications, and Internet commerce. I based my choices in the market on research and advice from individuals who know the business much better than I know it. While my hopes were high, many of my choices were still speculative, merely guesses where I could not predict with absolute certainty which direction interest rates and the market would go. Our hope in Christ is not based on conjecture. We can know with certainty that the investment may be large, but the dividends are worth it.

God knows how incredibly weak we may be in living a Christian life. God also knows that at times we may be at a loss for words when we try to pray. Clarence Jordan says, "We don't know beans about praying."[7] However, as Jordan says, God's Spirit X-rays our hearts and intercedes for us in ways we cannot imagine.[8]

Maria was asked by her Sunday School teacher to write a short letter to God. Maria, who is 7, wrote, "Dear God: I think about You sometimes even when I'm not praying." Maybe we are praying even when we don't call it that. I think God appreciates those thoughts even when we don't articulate them with words.

We are incredibly limited by words. You've probably had the uneasy experience of visiting, writing, or calling someone who has lost a loved one. If you are like I am in these situations, you may have felt awkward and incredibly inadequate. However, it's not the words but the gesture that is most important. As in our condolences, it's the intent, not the words of our prayers, that is the important thing. When we are at a loss for words, the Spirit directs and interprets our fumbling, inarticulate prayers to bring them in line with the will of God because at times we confuse what we want with what we and the world need. Maybe our most earnest prayers involve no words but only guttural utterances or maybe just images. Romans 8:26 points out that the Spirit groans and sighs for us when we cannot find the words to say. Being a part of God's family guarantees us this gift.

In that same Sunday School class, Juan's prayer went like this: "Dear God: If You watch me in church on Sunday, I'll show you my new shoes." Little Juan associated God's presence and watchful eye with a place—church. Too often we forget that our thoughts and conversations with God should be a continuous part of everyday life, not just an occasion at certain points in the day or week.

Our relationship with God should be as natural and ongoing as breathing.

Questions for personal reflection

1. How do you qualify for being a daughter of God, and what are your privileges and gospel responsibilities as a member of God's family?
2. Describe what you think the dynamics of Jesus' family were like.
3. How does hope help you through suffering?
4. Have you ever been unable to pray? Have you experienced God's Spirit uttering a prayer on your behalf? Do you think you are aware when this happens?
5. What does this passage mean as it relates to intercessory prayer? How do our prayers for others when they are exhausted or weary in spirit give them hope?

Responsible to God's purpose

Read Romans 8:28–30. Paul assures us that our worse struggles and sufferings can become blessings. Although bad things will inevitably happen to good people, God can transform that. We can be assured of God's cooperation with us in *all things*. God will work with us no matter what the conditions or circumstances, even when we botch things up or when disaster comes our way.

God wants us to be transformed into Christ's image in much the same way an ordinary chrysalis is transformed into a radiant butterfly. For that to happen, we must develop a new attitude and a willing relationship with God. As Dale Moody says, "Salvation is a walk, not a hop with God holding man by the hair of his head!"[9] Part of this involves seeing ourselves as made in God's image, gifted and capable. This means that while we must be realistic, we must also seize the day with confidence not only in God but also in ourselves. We must be willing for God to transform us as we are called to keep our end of the bargain.

Read Romans 8:31–39 and notice the things against which God protects us. What is your greatest fear? If we have received the gift of God's only Son, surely you can count on God to comfort you even in the scariest situations. Goodness and strength can flourish in the most surprising places against the most difficult obstacles. Even the weak at times emerge victorious against odds that seem overwhelming. We can emerge from the fire of tragedy with a newfound strength. "The power which robs misfortune of its sting and transforms it into a blessing is the power of love."[10]

I don't know about you, but often I have difficulty seeing what good can come out of some tragedies. The rape of my aunt, the Oklahoma City bombing, the massacre at Columbine High School, and the ethnic cleansings abroad make us search for answers. Sometimes the voice of God is clear, but sometimes we may misinterpret or mistake what we hear. In September 1999, Wedgwood Baptist Church in Fort Worth, Texas, suffered a horrendous tragedy. A disturbed gunman walked into the church and opened fire killing seven people and injuring seven others before taking his own life. Even the sanctity of this fine church was not immune to disaster.

In the aftermath of that tragedy, the church was inundated with an amazing outpouring of love and support, and many people decided to become Christians. These are just the beginning of the ways God worked following the shooting. God was there to pick up the pieces and to help heal those whose lives were changed forever. Some saw God at work even during the shooting, one person reporting that the gunman fired 100 bullets into a crowd of more than 400 hitting only 14. A person in my Sunday School class responded, "*Only* 14! My word! This was not much comfort to those who *were* hit. Why didn't God spare them? All that statistic tells me is that the gunman was just a bad shot."

One man saw the shooting as providential. He said he had prayed that God would do whatever it took to expand the ministry of that church. While people once had difficulty finding the church, the man said that now almost everyone in the world knows exactly where it is. Do you take this man's comment to mean that God answered his prayer by having all those people shot to get the church publicity? How do you interpret this comment? What do you believe about God's will in these situations?

We must exercise care in reading and interpreting Scripture. No doubt the losses and tragedies we face are faith influences, sometimes positive ones and sometimes negative ones. But Paul does not say that God makes a bad thing happen so that good can come out of it. Nothing that is of God is tainted. Instead he says that even in our darkest days, God will sustain us. While God may not need our help, how much gospel responsibility do we each have in helping something good come out of something bad?

The love of Christ can transform evil, pain, and suffering into something positive. Our loyalty to Christ ensures that nothing can defeat us. We can be secure, sure that our policy premium has been paid in full. God's grace covers whatever calamity arises both now and in the future. Paul says that even powers over which we have no control cannot terrorize us, that nothing can separate us from the love of God in Christ. That love prompts each of us to a gospel responsibility. Our praying for victims of disaster and others who encounter loss then moves us to action. After praying for flood victims in

North Carolina, we then go to them with supplies, helping hands, and encouragement.

The direction in which God's love takes us is no accident, but is a wonderfully conceived plan. Maybe it moves us to prepare a meal for a grieving family, to send Christmas boxes to children in Bosnia, or to go to Guatemala to rebuild flood-ravaged homes. God wants us to grow more like Christ, finally achieving the final purpose of God. The pilgrimage, though agonizing at times, has a huge payoff, a family reunion with all our adopted siblings.

We have much to look forward to. Paul Achtemeier says, "We are like people on a drought-parched land, who hear the distant thunder of the approaching storm."[11] God quenches our thirst in abundant amounts. When Jesus fed the multitudes in Matthew 14:13–21, He had food left over. Like the loaves and fish on that day, God's love and care today do not have to be rationed. These things are ours for the asking. Thanks be to God.

Questions for personal reflection

1. How hard is it for you to trust that God works good in *all things*, even those that seem disastrous? Name one time in your life when calamity turned out to be a blessing.
2. What does *called* mean, as it is explained in Romans 8:28–30. Are some people not called?
3. What do you believe about God's will in disasters? What do Paul's words offer us here?
4. Can you understand why some people never recover spiritually from a tragedy? Explain how this might be a negative faith influence for them.

[1]Mary C. Boys, *Educating in Faith: Maps and Visions* (San Francisco: Harper and Row, 1989; reprint, Kansas City, MO: Sheed and Ward, [1993?]).

[2]Richard Cimino and Don Lattin, *Shopping for Faith: American Religion in the New Millennium* (San Francisco: Jossey-Bass, 1998), 46, citing Kevin Culligan, "Are We Wired for God?" *America,* March 22, 1997, 23–24.

[3]Paul J. Achtemeier, *Romans,* vol. in *Interpretation: A Bible Commentary for Teaching and Preaching* (Louisville, KY: John Knox Press, 1985), 136–37.

[4]Ibid., 137.

[5]Tisa Lewis, "Spiritual Confessions of a Searching Boomer" (working title; unpublished manuscript), 91.

[6]Beverly Roberts Gaventa, "Romans," in *The Women's Bible Commentary,* ed. Carol A. Newsom and Sharon H. Ringe (Louisville, KY: Westminster/John Knox Press, 1992), 318.

[7]Clarence Jordan, *The Cotton Patch Version of Paul's Epistles* (New York: Association Press, 1968), 219.

[8]Ibid.

[9]Clifton J. Allen, ed., *The Broadman Bible Commentary* (Nashville: Broadman Press, 1970), 10:222.

[10]George Arthur Buttrick, ed., *The Interpreter's Bible* (Nashville: Abingdon Press, 1978), 9:532.

[11]Achtemeier, *Romans,* 148.

7

God's Call Fulfills God's Promises

Romans 9–10

From my earliest recollections, church and the Bible were a part of my life, important faith influences. On Sunday mornings we had several rituals around my house. At Sunday School, Myra Beth Senterfeit would usually tell me I smelled like fried chicken because at the crack of dawn, my mother was up cooking Sunday dinner which often consisted of, among other things, green beans, potato salad, homemade macaroni pie, and, of course, fried chicken. In the summer months when the garden was producing, we added fresh sliced tomatoes, cucumbers, and stewed squash to the menu. German chocolate cake, pecan pie, banana pudding from scratch, strawberry shortcake, and a great congealed salad often ended our afterchurch meal. These fantastic desserts were many times contributed by my grandmama who along with my granddaddy ate nearly every Sunday dinner with us.

Before church each Sunday morning, with no exceptions, I closely watched my daddy put the money in the offering envelopes and then write something on the outside. When I got old enough to write (legibly!), this became my job. Daddy would put the money out for me and I would fill out the envelopes. Then we'd all load up in the car, and after my parents, Debbie, John, and I had all gone to Sunday School, we went to "big church." The back row on the right-hand side was our row; still is. How that got started, I'm not real sure, but nobody else sat there except Grandmama and Granddaddy Temples. I usually sat by Granddaddy who had probably smoked a cigar before he came in. He and I made quite a pair, fried chicken and cigar smoke.

I also had a job in big church and that was to keep Granddaddy awake. You see, he had a little snoring problem, and you know how that can be in the middle of John 3:16. One Sunday when I caught him, as he would say, resting his eyes, I dutifully nudged him to wake him from a Sunday morning nap. After church that Sunday he gently told me (he was a very gentle man) not to keep punching him during the morning prayer.

Back in 1959 for Christmas, Grandmama and Granddaddy gave my sister and me new Bibles with a picture of Jesus and the little children on the front. I loved that picture so much because Jesus was stretching out his hands for the little children to come to Him. Inside were several other wonderful pictures that often entertained me during the parts of the sermon that were over my head. I looked at these great pictures of Jesus and the moneychangers, the ark, Moses, and David and Goliath nearly every Sunday. These pictures made it easy to visualize certain stories, but there were lots of things in that Bible that I did not understand. The biggest question I had was, What does all of this stuff that happened so long ago have to do with me?

In his commentary on Romans, Dale Moody points out that a danger exists in asking what Paul has to say to us today before asking what he had to say to the people of his day and his culture.[1] While the Word of God contains the same truth today as it did in Paul's day, many of the circumstances were different. Now I must admit to you that one of my least favorite subjects in school was history. As much of a movie fanatic as I am, I have to be highly motivated to watch a period piece, at least anything before the 1950s when I was born. Selfishly I want to be able to put myself right into the shoes of the characters, and this gets more difficult for me the older the history. For years this problem has plagued me and no doubt puts a kink in things as I try to study Scripture.

Having said that, I must say that chapters 9 and 10 of Romans are next to impossible to decipher unless we look at their historical context. Many of these historical factors were primary motives for why Paul expressed himself in certain ways and exercised such care. We must keep in mind the controversy at the time that was raging over (1) how Christians related to Jewish law and (2) the place of the Jews in God's plan.[2]

Paul, himself a Jew, likely wrote chapters 9 through 11 of Romans as a sermon, according to C. H. Dodd.[3] Romans 9:1 begins a new section, a carefully written independent unit in which Paul turns his full attention to those in the Jewish community who have rejected the gospel. He is about to travel to Palestine with an offering for the Jewish people there collected from predominantly Gentile churches. The collection serves as a bit of a peace offering that Paul hopes will bring reconciliation in the Gentile/Jewish controversy. Perhaps the reason Paul wrote this passage so carefully is because he is a little leery of the way he will be received and doesn't want to ruffle any feathers and offend the people in Rome. With great detail he explains his attitude toward Israel and his opinion of how the Jews, the Chosen People, fit into God's plan. Here Paul can't come across as despising his Jewish heritage because the church in Rome, which had positive feelings toward the Jews, might not have been pleased with a negative portrayal.[4]

You might already be asking as I asked as a child, What does this have to do with a white Baptist girl from Batesburg? How do I fit into this controversy between the Jews and the Gentiles that happened so long ago? Archibald M. Hunter has identified the theme of chapters 9 and 10 of Romans as the purpose of God in history,[5] no small effort! Now complete a little assignment and read Romans 9–10 before we go any further. You may have to read both chapters in several translations to get the gist of what Paul is saying. Look for verses that bring out this theme. Paul offers his belief that God has moved in history and has fulfilled promises through God's offer of grace.

Early in history, God selected and used the nation of Israel to fulfill God's purposes. In these passages from Romans, Paul shows how God has fulfilled the promises made to the Jewish community and has extended the offer of grace and salvation also to Gentiles. This is where we begin to fit in.

For many, the Jewish rejection of the gospel has called the promises of the Old Testament into question. How can God's promise of grace extend beyond the selected nation of Israel when Israel itself has rejected God's offer of grace? Paul uses this portion of the letter to the church at Rome to affirm the faithfulness of the promises of God and the offer of grace extended to his Jewish kinfolk. In presenting his arguments, Paul offers us renewed assurances that God's promises are trustworthy and challenging as we each choose individually to respond to the grace these promises offer.

Hunter's theme stated above seems a bit overwhelming to me. Now break down this overarching theme into some smaller, more manageable themes. Reread Romans 9–10, carefully marking words that indicate the following themes: God's faithfulness to all; God's offer of grace to Israel; individual accountability through belief and action.

Paul begins this section of verses by stating his devotion to his kinfolk. Again, maintaining a degree of loyalty to his roots, Paul points to several aspects of the Jewish heritage in which he takes great pride: the glory, the covenants, the law, worship, the promises, the patriarchs, and the Jewish heritage of Jesus (vv. 4–5). He identifies each of these as meaningful aspects of Jewish responses to God that have also found significant places in Christian expressions of worship and faith (vv. 6ff.). Paul points to each of these as evidence that God has not failed God's promises to the Jewish nation but has offered fulfillment of those promises in the person of Christ.

While Israel was the selected nation, as a nation it did not respond to the call of God. Although the result of Israel's unresponsiveness may *appear* to be the absence of God's mercy, Paul points out that God is not unjust (v. 14). God offers mercy (vv. 15–16). God cannot be faulted for Israel's rejection of the offer of grace. The responsibility for responding to the call of God lies within each individual. While the rejection of God's grace by Israel represents personal sadness for Paul, he does not release his people from their individual accountability toward God.

For years while I was in college and graduate school, I worked on the waterfront at Woman's Missionary Union® (WMU®) camps in South Carolina. Every summer in June when the spring semester was over, I would pack my clothes and books and head for about ten weeks of fellowship and fun with other young women my age along with hundreds of campers. Each week we were fortunate to have with us a home (North American) missionary or couple, and a foreign (international) missionary or couple. As you can imagine, we heard fascinating stories of how these missionaries had influenced and had been influenced by diverse communities from

Appalachia to Algeria. One story that sticks out in my mind helps me to understand a bit of what Paul may have felt and why some people are reluctant to accept Christ.

On one hot July afternoon between swimming groups, I remember sitting on the floating dock of Cedar Lake at Camp Rawls talking to the international missionary couple visiting us that week. While I cannot recall the name of the country where they served, I vividly remember how shocked I was when they told me how many of the Muslim people with whom they worked had accepted Christ in the seven years of their ministry. Two, only two, people had converted from Islam to Christianity! I was astounded that all of their efforts had yielded such sparse results. Not being able to imagine why people were not more receptive to the gospel, I asked the couple to what they would attribute this.

As I mentioned at the beginning of this chapter, all my life I had known nothing but Christianity. The couple told me to imagine that one day some strangers came into town from a different country. After getting to know the people in my community and learning our ways for quite a while, they proceeded to tell us that they had a message that would change our lives. Now most of the people in my community had always been Christians and felt that what they believed was true beyond doubt, and they were committed to the idea that nothing could ever change that belief. Our Messiah had come and would never be replaced by any other message.

The missionaries then asked: How long would it take to convince you and your Christian neighbors that the message they brought that you had never heard before was the one true message, that what you had believed all these decades was only part of the story? I couldn't really answer their question. The only thing I could think of as a young 19-year-old was, "Those folks might as well not waste their time on my people." I told them that I was beginning to see how difficult their job must have been and how difficult it must be for devout Muslims, Jews, or Buddhists as a people to accept something so radical and so unbelievable.

The next semester I took a course on Islamic civilization and became even more aware of just how devout many of these Muslims are. These people would put some of us Christians to shame with their faithfulness and devotion. And in my small mind I thought, "Maybe the Holy Spirit should just intervene and convict those nations." Paul would answer again that the individual is responsible for his or her own decision. However, in Romans 9, Paul's emphasis is on the *nation* of Israel not, not *individual* Israelites.

The nation of Israel had not responded to the call proclaiming the Christ and the gospel message, but the Gentiles had been included. Paul points out the irony that it was not the Gentile world, but Israel, that was seeking after righteousness; yet it was the Gentiles who heard and accepted God's offer of grace.

For centuries many people have misinterpreted Paul's words in 9:1–18 to mean that God has already picked who will be saved and who will perish, and we don't have any choice in the matter. This could not be further from the truth. I can understand why some people who have been fed a steady diet of this kind of talk and have had faith influences like this want nothing to do with religion. While Paul does continually stress the sovereignty of God, he never portrays this kind of message of doom for those unlucky souls. He is not saying this at all. Paul never says that one's decision to reject the gospel is willed, let alone predetermined by God.

Like Mary Boys's reference to mapmaking and as Moody points out, "Predestination means we know where we are going before we get there."[6] Let's contrast the ideas of predeterminism and predestination to get a better idea of what Paul is saying. According to Achtemeier, predetermined essentially means preprogrammed. Every idea and every action has been typed in or dictated so that the person has absolutely no control over thoughts or behavior.

You might compare this to the computer chip in your VCR. While VCRs at times do seem to have minds of their own, particularly when you've tried to record your favorite show, the machines cannot do anything that they have not been "told" to do. Predeterminism is not at all what Paul is referring to in chapter 9. Contrastingly, Achtemeier says that predestination merely sets the options for the outcome but doesn't dictate the course. Moreover, we must see here that fortunately for us, God is a God of mercy and grace; and as Achtemeier says, God deals with us not according to who *we* are but instead based on Who God is, our merciful Creator, Redeemer, and Sustainer.[7]

Questions for personal reflection

1. According to Romans 9:1–19, how do you think Paul felt about his Jewish heritage? God's faithfulness to God's promises? The mercy of God?
2. How would you describe the difference in predestination and predeterminism? How do those who hold to a doctrine of predeterminism see individual choice? What do you think of Paul's words concerning predestination?

Called to be God's vessels, God's influences

Read Romans 9:20–22 (TEV) carefully: "A clay pot does not ask the man who made it, 'Why did you make me like this?' After all, the man who makes the pots has the right to use the clay as he wishes, and to make two pots from the same lump of clay, one for special occasions, and the other for ordinary use." And the same is true of what God has done. These verses portray God as the Creator of vessels. The idea of vessel implies *purpose* and *usefulness* of the vessel as well as the *power* and *mercy* of the Creator. Vessels are always created with forethought and purpose. While individual vessel styles and roles may differ, their collective purpose is to serve the Creator. To question our purpose or to envy the purpose of others is to abandon our unique calling and to limit the kingdom of God.

This is hard medicine for me to swallow. My problem here is that I am incredibly limited by my humanness, especially in my sin of envy. In our attempts to understand God, we want to give God anthropomorphic, or human, form and can often understand God only in human terms. We have such a hard time understanding the big picture and God's intent because we want God to be like us, to make God in our image.

Nakia sees God *anthropomorphically,* although she, of course, would not use that word. She asks, "If God is so merciful, why didn't God make us all beautiful vessels, not some all humped over and lopsided with rough edges. Sometimes I think if my hair weren't kinky and my skin were white, the world might like me better." Here Nakia sounds a bit like Maya Angelou in *I Know Why the Caged Bird Sings* and goes on to say, "Sometimes I say to myself, 'You ugly nappy-headed black girl, God must've had a good laugh when He made this junk pile pot.'"

Now Nakia, who is actually quite a beautiful young woman, thinks she got the short end of the stick when it comes to vessel making. She is no junk pile pot. Not only is she beautiful; she is also brilliant and talented, even though influences in her life have made her feel otherwise.

Part of her discomfort is likely due to racial prejudice, but some may be attributed to pure, adolescent self-consciousness. As Nakia gains more and more confidence and maturity, she will begin to see that she is a fine vase and that God has big plans for her in the gospel responsibility department. But she will certainly need some encouragement, some good faith influences, along the way.

Paul reminds us that God accomplishes His work in the world through His vessels. In these creations, God reveals the riches of His glory to the world. God's willingness and ability (again, anthropomorphic terms) to use all available vessels to communicate to the world is a strong theme of this passage.

The preparation of the nation of Israel as a vessel of mercy was a special honor for the Jewish people; but when Israel was unable to respond to God through faith without law, God did not limit the call to the selected nation of Israel. The Gentiles who responded to God through their faith in Christ also became the vessels of God, and it was through their faithfulness that the gospel spread throughout the first-century world. As such they offered models for modern-day missions. They responded with excitement and commitment to the call of God through Christ. As faulty but willing vessels, they carried the gospel to the world.

Called from all races and cultures

The Jewish and Gentile worlds represented extremes in culture. Within the context of the New Testament, they represent different approaches to God. Read carefully Romans 9:31–32. Israel chose to retain her approach to God through the righteousness of the Law. Go back and read verse 30 carefully. The Gentile world had come to know God through the offer of grace through faith in Christ.

For Paul's audience the point is not lost that the unheeded call to the selected nation of Israel is then extended to the Gentiles, the very people for whom Israel had little regard (vv. 24–26). The great differences in Jewish and Gentile culture offer an excellent example of the diversity God uses. The cause of God crosses cultural barriers of all types. Neither God nor the gospel message can be confined to one set of cultural perceptions or practices.

White, middle-class Protestants do not have the market on truth. We can only know what we have experienced, and for some of us, myself included, our experience is quite limited. God transcends our finite understanding of culture, diversity, and difference. Through the gospel message our similarities of needs and desires, our commonality and communality as people of God are accentuated.

At a recent retreat in the snow-covered mountains of North Carolina, I discovered that a friend from my church and I share the same birth month and birth year. I am exactly one week older than he. I don't know about you, but when I find someone who was born at the same time as I, this provides a special bond. Now some people would say that my friend Wond and I have little in common. He is a black man from Ethiopia, and I am a white woman from Batesburg, South Carolina. But the more I learned about Wond during the retreat, the more I saw what we had in common. And the more I learned about Wond and his perspective on faith, the more I saw myself as a limited, myopic Baptist-born and Baptist-raised American who needs to listen and get fresh perspectives and insights from individuals who come from different backgrounds that are rich in faith influences.

Our differences become opportunities for celebrating the encompassing nature of God, and our fears of these differences are allayed. Inclusive by its very nature, the gospel is offered to all and therefore all cultures and races share in the responsibility of communicating the message of God to their world. In the process of our sharing and conversation, the world and the people in it become connected in extraordinary ways.

Israel did not share that perspective on inclusivity and this nation gives us the example of a people who in their exclusive approach to God's grace limit the effectiveness of the gospel. As Israel sought to approach God solely through a righteousness of the Law, they missed the righteousness of faith God offered. In Romans 9:33 Paul uses the familiar image of Christ as a rock of the faith. Through Israel's lack of faith in Christ, they stumbled.

Questions for personal reflection

1. Review Romans 9:20–30; then consult a good Bible dictionary, map, commentary, or concordance. What do you think Paul meant in his references to: Hosea (v. 25); Isaiah (v.27); Sodom and Gomorrah (v. 29)?
2. As you review Romans 9, what two major ideas do you find?
3. What diverse groups of people in your community have you failed to have contact with? What might those individuals teach you?

Accountable in our zeal

Romans 10 begins with an additional assertion of Paul's loyalty to his nation and offers his sincere hope that the Jewish nation's zeal for God will one day include acceptance of Christ. Read Romans 10:1–8 keeping in mind that verses 6–8 are based on Moses' words to the Israelites in Deuteronomy 30:12–14.[8] Paul does not dispute or discount the enthusiasm Israelites hold for the righteousness of God. Their zeal for God is not enough, however; it is lacking in a complete knowledge and understanding of God's message through Christ.

Bear with me as we do a bit of double-talk. Loving goodness versus loving goodness—what is the difference and which is better? *Loving goodness* with *loving* as a verb would be similar to having zeal for goodness. This is not all bad, but Paul says it is not enough. However, *loving goodness* with *loving* as an adjective is more in line with the message of Christ. If we possess loving goodness, we reflect the Word Incarnate rather than just the words. You probably are familiar with people who seem to love the Bible more than wanting to be like Jesus. Our participation in the work of God needs to be enthusiastic; but our enthusiasm needs to be based on a correct understanding of the purpose and person of Christ. In all our enthusiasm for God, we must not substitute zeal for Christlike attitudes, understanding, knowledge, and meaningful action.

Questions for personal reflection

1. As Paul understands it, what was wrong with Jewish zeal?
2. Name some times in your life with you have seen misdirected zeal.
3. What are some examples of loving goodness versus loving goodness?

Accountable in our words

For Paul, crucial to Israel's salvation is an understanding of righteousness that depends on faith in God rather than their own righteousness. We express our beliefs as an act of individual accountability. Read Romans 10:8–11. Our genuine beliefs support our actions. The confession that Jesus is Lord must be accompanied by the belief that He is Lord. Belief and confession must be integrated into a single expression of faith. To believe without expressing the belief abandons one's responsibility as a vessel of God's mercy. To confess without belief is meaningless. This might be like the difference in saying the Lord's Prayer versus praying the Lord's Prayer.

Verses 9–10 here are Paul's interpretation of Deuteronomy 30:14. Nakia, now having read much of what Paul has to say in Romans, asks, "Why does Paul keep quoting from the Law in the Old Testament? I thought when Jesus was born, He was the Word, and the Law was fulfilled. Why can't we just look to Jesus?" Achtemeier answers Nakia's very good questions when he says that Paul keeps reiterating the Law because while Christ has made clear the Law's purpose, the Law now helps illuminate the Word now made Flesh. Christ is the fulfillment of the Law, but the Law aids us in understanding our relationship to God through Christ.[9]

Questions for personal reflection

1. How are you accountable to God for the words you speak?
2. Do you believe certain other Christians are more accountable or less accountable than you are? Why or why not?

Equal salvation for all

Understanding belief and confession as a single event leads to Paul's next point: There is equal salvation for all. God does not offer the Jews one kind of salvation and the Gentiles another. Read carefully Romans 10:12–13.

Notice that God offers the call to salvation to everyone, Jew and Gentile alike. At this point the differences that identify persons by gender, race, age, or culture all disappear. The call to faithfulness is the same and the individual accountability to respond to the call is the same. Each of us is accountable to bear witness and reflect the gospel message in our lives, no matter where we live or what our circumstances are. Individually these represent small reflections of the grace of God; collectively they represent the work of God in our world.

Accountable to witness and spread the gospel

Again in an ironic tone, Paul traces the responsibility the Jews have for receiving the gospel. Read verses 10:14–21. The Jews had opportunity to hear, to understand, and to believe; therefore, the responsibility for not accepting was their own. The Gentiles were without the Jewish experience of God's promises, but they heard, believed, and acted upon their faith. What then could be Israel's excuse? The Gentiles not only had heard the word of the gospel but also had taken responsibility for giving witness of their faith. With hearing and belief come the responsibilities for sharing the gospel with others. "We've a story to tell to the nations," and that story must be told in word and deed.

Paul ends the chapter with a quote from Isaiah that echoes God's desire for the people of Israel to respond to the abundant grace given to them. Again, we see God as anthropomorphic, in human form, and we are left with the image of the outstretched hands of a beckoning God, just like the hands of Jesus with the little children on the front of that Bible I got in 1959. We also have the answer to that question I asked as a child at the beginning of this chapter, What does all of this stuff that happened so long ago have to do with me? Those outstretched hands are pretty clear.

Questions for personal reflection

1. How is Romans 10:14 a mission statement?
2. Who are the people with beautiful feet (v. 15 NRSV)? Who are they today?
3. What early childhood influences cause you to shy away from people who are different from you? How does your church encourage dialogue among groups of people who on the outside look different or who may have different beliefs? Do you believe that such dialogue can help bring about peace in your community and around the world?

[1]Clifton J. Allen, ed., *The Broadman Bible Commentary* (Nashville: Broadman Press, 1970), 10:160.
[2]C. Milo Connick, *The New Testament: An Introduction to Its History, Literature, and Thought,* 2nd ed. (Belmont, CA: Wadsworth, 1978), 308.
[3]C. H. Dodd, *The Epistle to the Romans* (New York: Harper and Row, 1932), 148–50, quoted in Connick, *New Testament,* 308.
[4]Connick, *New Testament,* 308.
[5]Archibald M. Hunter, *Introducing the New Testament*, 2nd ed., rev. and exp. (Philadelphia: Westminster Press, 1957), 94.
[6]Allen, *Broadman Bible Commentary*, 10:222.
[7]Paul J. Achtemeier, *Romans*, vol. in *Interpretation: A Bible Commentary for Teaching and Preaching* (Louisville, KY: John Knox Press, 1985), 155–64.
[8]Ibid., 169.
[9]Ibid., 169–70.

8

God's Call Is Sure

Romans 11

Sluggish souls, olive branches, and roots—we can identify with theses images from Paul in Romans 11. Clarence Jordan also uses vivid, sometimes even humorous imagery in his contemporary *Cotton Patch Version of Paul's Epistles* and helps us better understand what Paul is saying to us in chapter 11 of Romans. These images are important to someone who is as visually oriented as I am, especially when looking at ideas that are so abstract. We will look at how Jordan describes some of these abstract concepts that Paul presents, such as fairness, responsibility, and grace.

"At issue is the fairness of God."[1] Achtemeier immediately points out what many of us may be thinking after reading previous chapters of Romans where we see God making beautiful vessels versus homely pots, choosing some and not choosing others, and hardening the hearts of one group while showing mercy on another. In chapter 11, Paul continues with similar themes causing us to ask similar questions.

Just as Paul ended the previous chapter, he begins chapter 11 with an assertion of the sustained grace of God for the nation of Israel. The responsibility for response to this continued grace is one way in which we, like the nation of Israel, are accountable to the call of

God. Read Romans 11:1–6 and look for Paul's insistence that God remains faithful to all promises of grace. Israel had neglected to respond to this call, but it was not God's fault. God offers grace.

Paul offers himself as an example of the faithfulness of God—as one who belongs to the elect nation of Israel. Paul was of the same Jewish heritage, but he chose to participate in God's offer of grace. For Paul this is evidence that God has been faithful to the offer of grace. The responsibility for Israel's separation from God rests with Israel.

Questions for personal reflection

1. Some of the words in this passage refer to 1 Kings 19. Read that Old Testament chapter (especially vv. 10,14). What important facts do you find there?
2. Why do you think Paul quoted from 1 Kings 19?

Accountable to a sovereign God

Read Romans 11:7–22. In this passage Paul uses several images to emphasize the sovereignty of God in the call to the Jews and Gentiles. Since the offer of grace comes from God, we are accountable to God in our responses. Through God's offer of grace to all people, we can understand God's sovereignty. Only one with complete and absolute power can make a real offer of grace. Paul does not excuse those who reject the offer of God's grace but describes their situation as "hardened" to the things of God.

Paul makes it clear in verses 1 and 2 that God did not reject Israel. Drawing from the Old Testament (Deut. 29:4; Psalm 69:22–23*a*; Isa. 6:9; 29:10; Jer. 5:21), Paul cites reasons for Israel's lack of response to God's grace. As in many cases, the neglect of a gift results in the forfeit of the gift. The gift giver is not responsible for the result; instead, those who choose to neglect the gift must suffer the consequences of their actions.

One of my faults is that I sometimes try to look for a scapegoat when something doesn't work out for me. When I moved into my house, a friend of mine gave me a great sago palm along specific instructions for its care. After about a month, the branches started turning yellow; and before long, the whole thing was pretty much, well, dead. For a long time I just kept the dead thing, not wanting to throw it out especially since it had been a gift. Maybe I was also in a bit of denial of my carelessness and neglect. I finally accepted that it wasn't going to turn green again and got rid of it. Disappointed and a bit aggravated that my friend had given me this plant that had died on me, I called her and told her about it, almost blaming her for the sago's demise. She asked me if I had followed her instructions. "Well, no, not exactly." As with God and the people of Israel, the gift giver was not responsible for the result. Instead, I, who chose to neglect my gift, was to blame for the consequences of my actions, or the lack thereof.

The imagery Paul uses in verse 8 (NRSV) is "a sluggish spirit," or as Clarence Jordan calls it, "a sleepy spirit,"[2] to suggest the numbness which characterizes Israel's response to God. Israel had been rejecting God for so long that she had become numb to the call of God. This is especially poignant as Israel was God's select people.

Every fall when I teach a class on faith development, I usually include a section on discipline and how the ways that we discipline our children can have influences on their faith. When I teach this class, I always think back to the time that I was a very little girl to remember what kinds of discipline my parents used in my family. I remember one time my sister Debbie and I got in trouble for something fairly minor, unlike the time when she was 6 and I was 4 and we got caught trying to smoke a cigarette that we had swiped out of my granddaddy's store! Although I don't remember what the offense was this time, it must not have been as bad as the smoking incident because, unlike the spanking we got for that, this time our parents just sent us to the room we shared. We were supposed to think about what we had done wrong until my parents came back to get us. Within minutes, Debbie and I had fallen asleep, and when my parents came back to ask us what we had thought about our crime, obviously we couldn't say much. Needless to say, my parents had to change their discipline tactics because while I don't remember this, apparently Debbie and I *always* fell asleep immediately when we were sent to our rooms. Like those sleepy spirits that Paul refers to in verse 8, we were numb to our waywardness.

A second quotation (vv. 9–10) captures the idea of a snare or trap set to catch something hunted. Paul's reference (from David's Psalm 69:22–23*a*) is that each year as the nation of Israel gathered to share in a religious feast, she was "unaware of a coming catastrophe growing out of her rejection"[3] of the Messiah. So as the Israelites gathered to worship, they were unaware of the consequences of their neglect.

Read carefully Romans 11:11–16 and look for references to the Gentiles (non-Jews). Since Israel has rejected God's offer of grace through Christ, Paul turned his own ministry to the Gentiles in hopes that the promise of God may be fulfilled through them. If this were in America it might look something like this: Clarence Jordan's translation, putting this in present-day Washington, says that "because of their failure the Christian faith was sent to the unchurched, so as to get the WAP's [white American

Protestants] on the ball."[4] Then we get a preview of the next analogy of grafted branches that Paul uses.

In Romans 11:17–24, Paul uses the image of an olive tree. As gardeners break off branches so that they can graft on other branches to produce fruit, they are always aware of the root that supports the branches. In a similar way, the unbelieving Jews have been "plucked off" due to their unbelief. In their place, believing Gentiles have been "grafted" into the kingdom. Belief in the person and work of Christ is the basis for both of these actions. Keep in mind that Israel's failure to respond to God is just a temporary situation. God has the power to graft the Israelite branches back on, to reverse the process. Since their disbelief is partial and temporary, Paul finds hope for the eventual fulfillment of God's promises through Israel. Neither Jew nor Gentile has earned the right of their position on the olive tree; rather their inclusion is based solely on a response of faith to the offer of God's grace. But surely if God decides to graft the original Jewish branches back on, they will have the same status as the Gentile branches, especially because the Jewish branches were there to begin with.

Paul says that the promise of God will be fulfilled as Israel eventually responds to the salvation God offers. The gifts and the call of God are irrevocable. The fulfillment of time will see the fulfillment of these promises.

Questions for personal reflection

1. How are you accountable to a sovereign God? Give some examples of ways Christians can be hardened to the things of God.

2. What kind of olive branch are you? Are you in danger of being plucked off, or is your place on the olive tree

secure? How different can the branch be before the tree rejects it?

Accountable in a covenant relationship

Read Romans 11:23–29 and search for Paul's thoughts about God's establishing a covenant. The promises of God are based on a continued relationship of faith in Christ. The offer of grace is based on God's covenant with God's people. The covenant relationship implies a relationship that is not static or settled at any one point in history; rather, it requires continued attention and a renewed sense of commitment. For Jewish and Gentile believers this relationship must be renewed through continued faith and accountability. For those who do not yet believe, they still have the opportunity for a faith relationship, once they uncover the mysteries of God.

Paul warns those who have recently received the message of the gospel (the Gentiles) that they have not replaced God's original call to the Jewish nation: "For if God did not spare the natural branches, perhaps he will not spare you" (v. 21). Paul says that we must continue in kindness; otherwise we too will be cut off (v. 22). Our relationship is one of faith and requires continued growth and maturity, care and nurture. We must not allow our initial steps in faith to characterize our continued relationship with God. Just because we think we have arrived, we must not become complacent. Grace is free, but it is not cheap. And grace does not give us permission to do anything our Freudian id tells us to.

During my first few summers of work at Camp Rawls, the old WMU camp in South Carolina, I was determined to help lead as many young, impressionable girls to Christ as I possibly could. Just Get Them Down the Aisle was my motto, and I felt that if they cried a lot in the process, then they must have really been affected and we must have really done our job. Get them saved because you never know what might happen to them on the way back to their homes. These children were anywhere from 8 to 18, depending on the week, and everything some of us did in our nightly devotions led up to the last night of chapel where they had an invitation to receive Christ as their personal Lord and Savior. Now don't get me wrong. We also were intent on showing Christ's love and teaching the importance of loving God and our neighbors. But when it came to the big night, souls were at stake. I loved that night; and some of us thought if we could just get those girls to "walk the aisle," then we could be assured that they would escape the fires of hell and go to heaven.

What is wrong with this picture, and what does it have to do with what Paul is saying in these passages? Surely God wished salvation for those little girls, but several things were wrong with my young Christian perspective. First of all, I was basing the success of each week on the number of girls who prayed that prayer and the amount of emotion they expressed. Also, when I would counsel with the children who had come forward, I would say after they had asked Jesus into their hearts, "That's all you have to do. You are a Christian now. It's that easy." Well, it is not always that easy.

Barbara White, one of the camp directors, had a much more mature faith and theological training that most of us didn't. She worked diligently to help us understand the need for follow-up with these girls and the need to help them understand that their decision to follow Christ required responsibility and real commitment, that it was just the beginning of a sometimes difficult journey. Many of us staffers at first thought Barbara must not have understood the need to get those girls saved, to assure them of their rightful place in heaven. But as Paul says in Romans 11, grace does not mean that we can now do as we please. We have no God-given rights, only God-given love and mercy; and we are called to reflect that mercy toward others (Matt. 5:7). Barbara's influence helped us to see that gospel responsibility involves much more than "getting them down the aisle."

Moving back to the metaphor of the branches, Paul warns us against anti-Semitism. The Gentiles should not think that they are so "high and mighty" with their noses in the air, better than the Jews. In other words, the Gentiles should have respect for the Jews. Essentially he is saying that the Jews really have more of a right to be on the olive tree than the Gentiles do, especially since the Jews were there first (v. 24). The Gentiles shouldn't get all self-righteous thinking that they have *any* right to be grafted onto the tree in the first place.

One of my students recently experienced something back home that might help illustrate this situation. When Jon left for college, his parents decided to rent out his bedroom. Actually, they didn't really rent it; they just let Randy, a friend of the family, stay there because he had lost his job due to an embezzlement charge. Jon went home for summer vacation after his junior year, thinking that Randy was "back on his feet" again. He fully intended to move back into his room so that he could complete an internship in his hometown and save some money. To his surprise, embezzling Randy was still mooching off Jon's gracious parents; and, needless to say, his room was still occupied. Randy didn't deserve Jon's room. After all, Jon was there first. But Randy thought that since Jon had given it up, he would just stay. He should have realized that he had no right, especially since he was staying there rent-free and the room belonged to Jon.

Obviously the Gentiles were a bit like Randy. He should respect the fact that Jon had a right to his room by nature of his birth. But the family solved the problem by letting Jon back into his room; Randy reluctantly agreed to take the room over the garage. In this case the house, or the olive tree, was big enough for everybody, but certainly Jon had more of a right to live there than Randy did. This illustration breaks down at several points, first because Paul does not imply that the Gentiles are embezzlers or anything of the like. But it reinforces the idea that Gentiles should respect the Jews, especially since they are from the human family of Jesus. Spreading the good news to the Jews for Paul is essentially "recalling members of the family to their own home."[5]

Called under God's mercy and glory

Read Romans 11:30–36. God called the selected nation of Israel to faithfulness and offered them mercy, but after their unresponsiveness, He extended the gospel message and its accompanying mercy to the Gentile people. Paul offers this sequence of events as an example of God's sustained call. God's mercy is available to all, but all will not accept the invitation to receive God's mercy. God's mercy represents the path to salvation. The call of mercy is one which cannot be earned, but one which demands an earnest commitment.

As people called under God's mercy, we are called to remember the generous offer of God through Christ to us. We are called to respond faithfully in ways that express a genuine understanding of the nature of mercy. Thus the argument that opened the beginning of the epistle with the condemnation of all, closes with the gist of the whole chapter, God's mercy upon all will prevail.

Paul seems to be trying to promote unity in the midst of diversity in Romans 11:33–36. These verses are a doxology, a written expression of praise to God, bringing together both Greek (Gentile) and Hebrew (Jewish) ideas. Verses 34–35 are a composite of Old Testament passages incorporating lines of Hebrew poetry asking two interesting questions, almost amusing ones. Paraphrasing Clarence Jordan here we're asked if we are so haughty to think that we have probed God's mind, or been God's psychiatrist, or if we have ever made God a loan.[6] As a child who is always trying to figure God out, Nakia is very intrigued by these questions. She says, "Don't we all try to give God advice? We say, 'God, fix this and heal that.' We say, 'God, so-and-so needs food, and give that country peace.' Don't you think God already knows about that stuff? And in the process, we don't even ask the Spirit to lead us before we start those prayers. Sounds to me like we *do* try to boss God around and act like we're God's counselor or something." She continues, "And sometimes I think we do think God owes us something for what we have done, like when we help poor people and want to be blessed for it, and blessed *real* well. I think we do want God to give us back our deposit, and with interest, like we don't even understand that God gave us everything in the first place." Nakia may be right that many of us act as though we know better than God. But obviously God doesn't need advice from us nor has God received or needed a loan from us.

As mentioned previously, in verses 33–36 Paul cleverly brings together Hebrew and Greek tradition. In verse 33, the depth, riches, wisdom, and knowledge refer to the breadth of God as represented through the person of Christ, using images from Hellenistic (Greek) mysticism. Verse 33*b* draws from Hebrew ideas of the mysteries of God in the second line. The third line echoes Greek ideas of God as "the ground, guide, and goal of all things." Then the last line of the doxology is once again Hebrew.[7] Lines 1 and 3 then reflect Greek influence while lines 2 and 4 show a Hebrew flavor. So in a chapter that has sought to reconcile the Jewish and Gentile positions in the kingdom of God, Paul ends with a praise to God that incorporates poetry from each tradition.

Like Paul's attempt at reconciliation for two groups of people who were at odds, we have a gospel responsibility to be peacemakers (Matt. 5:9) and to celebrate diversity. Paul is not saying that we should all be alike. As in nature as ecological studies tell us, we are a healthier people if variety is present among us. Cultural differences bring color, texture, and depth to our understanding of God and the world. If God had wanted us to all look alike and be alike, He would have created us so. The Romans seemed to understand this very well and as a civilization lasted quite a long time. But many of us act as though we would be more comfortable if we could work with, play with, learn with, and worship with people who are just like us.

The twenty-first century has brought with it many challenges, one of which is to learn to live together in harmony. Some of us have difficulty doing this in our own families, much less with people of other socioeconomic groups, races, and ethnic groups. We must love each other or die. Time and time again, generation after generation, we've seen what happens when we don't practice this simple commandment that Jesus gave in Matthew, Mark, and Luke. "Love your neighbor as yourself," found in Luke 10 is followed with Jesus' definition of neighbor—the parable of the good Samaritan. And in the twenty-first century we must be more and more inclusive in our definition of neighbor. Our idea of who our neighbor is must get broader and more encompassing than ever. In so doing we can proclaim Paul's last sentence of the chapter: "To him be the glory forever. Amen."

Questions for personal reflection

1. Do you prefer to work, learn, and worship with people who are like you? Why or why not? Do you believe that you should change your thoughts on this?
2. How might you consciously and directly express a broader definition of who your neighbor is?
3. What are the groups in your neighborhood that could be compared to the Jews and the Gentiles?
4. Do you praise God daily? List some way that you can praise God.

[1]Paul J. Achtemeier, *Romans: Interpretation: A Bible Commentary for Teaching and Preaching* (Louisville, KY: John Knox Press, 1985), 178.
[2]Clarence Jordan, *The Cotton Patch Version of Paul's Epistles* (New York: Association Press, 1968), 35.
[3]Clifton J. Allen, ed., *The Broadman Bible Commentary* (Nashville: Broadman Press, 1970), 10:241.
[4]Jordan, *Cotton Patch Version,* 36.
[5]Achtemeier, *Romans,* 185.
[6]Jordan, *Cotton Patch Version,* 37.
[7]Allen, *Broadman Bible Commentary,* 10:247.

9

Gifts Accompany God's Call

Romans 12

Views of religiosity in America are changing, some better and some questionable. Rather than being a nation of "dwellers" as we were in the 1950s, we have become a nation of "seekers" and movers. Mobility has certainly increased and jobs call us to make many more moves than in the past; as a result, we sometimes have difficulty feeling rooted in any one place. In all of this moving, many people are more interested in "practicing" the gospel than in the "practices" of any one church or denomination.[1]

Postdenominational has been used to describe the fact that many people are now more interested in the programs provided for their children, the opportunities to serve, and fellowship with people of similar social values than they are in being loyal to a particular church or denomination. Most studies of baby boomers, those people born between 1946 and 1964, show declining church attendance and less connection to specific church teachings. This does not mean that they believe in God any less, but they just choose to worship alone or meditate rather than worshiping with others.[2] Times change and call for fresh ideas and new perspectives. While some people would rather return to the "good old days" of

Ward and June Cleaver or Ozzie and Harriet Nelson, as Tom Beaudoin pointed out in chapter 2, Generation Xers and many of us who are not so young are not satisfied with the way things have always been.

"Give me something practical, something I can use right now. And make it relevant." These words ring through the halls of academia as students seek something that they can chew on, something that will improve their lives. Often their reaction is to the old, tired lectures of professors whose notes have become yellow with year after year of the same old stuff. Others react to the fact that they just can't seem to get the connection between background information and actual practice.

Just as he did in his letters to the Galatians, Colossians, and Thessalonians, Paul begins his letter to the Romans with a discourse on doctrine. Now he will begin to move his emphasis to practical issues, ethical issues, what those restless students in my classes call for. Romans 12 marks the beginning of such an emphasis. This chapter of Romans also begins the final section of Paul's letter to the Christians at Rome where he presents the general theme of the righteousness of God as based on the brotherhood and sisterhood of all Christians.

Gospel responsibility to use our bodies and minds

On the refrigerator in a church member's home, I recently saw a magnet with the words, *Take care of your body. If you don't, where will you live?* While I smiled when reading this, the words emphasized that not only must I eat nutritious foods and exercise regularly for good health but I also have a responsibility in maintaining the home of the Holy Spirit. Our bodies are the temple of God; and, I must admit, after just consuming too many slices of pepperoni and sausage pizza with extra cheese, this house needs some remodeling. But in the first verse of this chapter, as we will see, Paul is talking about more than just our bodies.

Romans 12:1–3 issues the appeal for us to present our whole selves to God. These verses identify the transformation of our lives in this world as a representation of the promises in the kingdom of God. Paul points to God's mercy (v. 1) as ample motivation and sufficiency to accomplish the transformation. Consider God's mercy in your own life. That mercy encompasses both the compassion of God and the life of Christ, which offers "a majestic model for mercies."[3]

An additional translation of *your bodies* in verse 1 reads "your very selves" (NEB) and represents the fullest expression of selfhood for Paul. The phrase *living sacrifice* points to the contrast between the dead bodies of animal sacrifices people offered in Paul's day and the new life of sacrificial love the Spirit creates. Why should we offer our very selves as living sacrifices to God? Paul indicates the purpose of this offer of the self is *spiritual worship*. He indicates this act of sacrifice is *holy* and *acceptable* (NRSV) to God. Paul's exhortation begins in verse 1 with the call to be accountable in the use of our bodies and minds as we use them and our whole selves to the service of the kingdom of God.

This emphasis on the internal aspects of worship and service contrasts with the external aspects of temple worship. While we may be tempted to interpret this spiritual worship as an activity lived out apart from the world, Paul is fully aware that we must live out our Christianity in our current world. The renewal of our minds and spirits will continually transform us in the kingdom of God. In New Testament literature, the mind represents more than our rational capabilities. The mind also "includes the personality viewed in its deepest aspects"[4] and our personal awareness.

Transformation. This is a powerful word that carries with it beautiful connotations. Clarence Jordan uses one of the most common metaphors we think of when we think of change for the better. He says, "And don't let the present age keep you in its cocoon. Instead, metamorphose into the new mind."[5] Researchers tell us that personality is fairly consistent as we age. With few exceptions, my classmates at my 25th high school reunion, while physically very different in many cases, were much the same in terms of personality. Betsy was her same outgoing, friendly self; and Myra, despite the recent death of her husband, Larry, was as witty as always. But I dare say that the *attitudes* of many of my classmates had changed dramatically, and often for the better. I found that many of us had been transformed in at least a couple of ways, freeing our minds of racial prejudice and economic pride that had once infected many of us as young, sheltered, and self-absorbed adolescents. The transformation process has a long way to go, but at least it has begun. Who knows what we'll see at our 50th reunion!

Often my students ask me, "How can we figure out God's will for our lives?" My students are primarily human services majors which means they plan to go into counseling, social work, or other helping professions. They genuinely want to know how God can use them; and, as we will see later, I as their advisor have a responsibility here. As God transforms and uses all aspects of our lives to their fullest, we will be able to "discern what is the will of God—what is good and acceptable and perfect" (v. 2 NRSV). Discerning involves testing. The New International Version translates the passage: "Then you will be able to test and approve what God's will is—his good, pleasing and perfect will." The test is to decide what is good, what is acceptable, and what is agreeable to God. Finding God's perfect will is finding ways to reach God's true goals for our lives.

For my students, part of this testing means that they must explore what is out there, what many avenues are available to explore. This exploration involves certainly prayerful searching, reading, class discussions, and research, but it also involves moving beyond the confines of the little mountain cove where our college is situated. They must go out of the gate of Montreat to see the larger world and its needs and not rest in the comfort and safety of the sometimes myopic and cloistered college campus.

Paul instructs each person to respond to God's call with grace, sober judgment, and faith. Read verse 3 and pick out the specific instructions God gives Christians. While we are responsible and accountable to God, we should not be so high-minded to think that our rebellion or lack of Christian action will disrupt the work of God. God is powerful enough to accomplish God's will without us, but God chooses to work through us as He gives us mercy and faith. Paul's reference to "the measure of faith that God has given" (v. 3) refers to "faith as a power to do certain things . . . not faith as the response to God's saving grace."[6] Once we, through faith, become Christians, we then exercise our faith in God to empower us to act, to follow God's will, to move outside the gate. In the words of the call to worship at my church recently, we do this "with hearts open to the love of God, with hands outstretched to one another, and with whole selves willing to accept the cost and joy of being Christ's disciples."

Questions for personal reflection (vv. 1–3)

1. Define Romans 12:1–3 in your own words. In what ways are each of us transformed?

2. How have you been transformed as God has changed your life in the last 5 years? Ten years? Twenty years?
3. In what ways do you express this transformation? What other areas of your life would be positively affected if a complete transformation took place?

Called to community

Once we understand the individual aspects of our faith in some sense of order and perspective, we can then participate in our faith as part of the cooperative effort of the community. Together with other Christians and those in our world seeking to serve and love others, we form one body with many aspects, many dimensions, and many capabilities.

This variety does not set us at cross-purposes with others, but allows us to work toward a common purpose: God's purpose. While Paul explains the image of *the body of Christ* in some of his other letters such as in Ephesians 4, this reference in Romans helps us to see individuals as *members of one another*. Read Romans 12:4–5 carefully.

This aspect of interdependence recognizes our responsibility to participate in the mission of the kingdom of God fully and yet it negates our total individualism, which is inappropriate for the purpose and work of the community of believers. We cannot be isolationists but must interact with others recognizing that without each other, we lack perspective and vision and are not capitalizing on all of the rich resources and variety that God has created. The old Gestalt adage, "The whole is more important than the sum of its parts," is certainly true here.

In her book, *The Bean Trees*, Barbara Kingsolver gives a wonderful example of the necessity of working together and depending on each other. She tells a South American story of a group of people who are dying of starvation because their diet consists of a delicious soup, but they only have spoons as long as mop handles with which to eat. Imagine trying to eat with a spoon that is four feet long. The interesting thing is another community of people seems to be thriving even though their circumstances are the same: the same wonderful soup and the same ridiculously long spoons. How could this be? The second community was thriving because instead of trying to eat with these unmanageable utensils, they were *feeding each other* with these long unwieldy spoons.[7] Working together has its advantages; and like the community who had not learned to do this, we too may perish if we don't find ways to work with each other.

Paul also uses this image of interdependence to emphasize the necessity of our horizontal participation in the kingdom of God. We look upward to God vertically; we look out to others horizontally. As Barbara Kingsolver has so wonderfully illustrated, God does not call us to function in isolation from others. At the very basis of a concept of missions must be our belief that God calls us to be in a service relationship, not only with Christ but also with other people. "Participation in Christ means participation in the lives of other Christians,"[8] and maybe even in the lives of those who are not.

In this changing world, we must also recognize the necessity and opportunity to work with people who are not Christians. In my hometown, I did not know anyone who was not Christian expect two families, one being the Bogos. The Bogos lived near my Grandmama and Granddaddy Temples, and Mrs. Bogo had been my expression teacher in the first and second grades. I liked her very much. She was the first Jew I had ever met and she helped me to see that some people, while not Christians, were kind, generous, and loving, much the way Jesus was. Early on I began to see that we have much to learn from people who are not necessarily from the same ethnic or religious background as we are. Jews, Muslims, Buddhists, and Hindus, while different in religious approach, often have similar values and desire to live in harmony, to live interdependently. We will look at this more closely in verses 18–21.

Questions for personal reflection (vv. 4–5)

1. What is necessary for a community to function well together?
2. Do you believe we have a gospel responsibility to look for commonality and work with those persons who might be of other faith traditions? If so, how do we go about this?

Responsible to use our gifts and love wastefully

In Romans 12:6–8, Paul recognizes the importance of a variety of gifts in a diverse community. The diversity of our participation in the work of Christ is not random. Instead, it is the visible expression of God's grace as God individually gifts us with particular functions so the ministry of the entire body might be accomplished. The focus of Paul's words seems to be that each person has particular gifts, all the gifts are the result of God's grace, and each person should use her gifts to accomplish God's purpose.

Jesus illustrated this perhaps as well as anyone. In Luke 19:11–27, when Jesus told the story of the master who entrusted a pound each to his servants, He wanted His followers to understand several things. First of all, we are not all responsible and accountable to God for the same things, but we are all accountable to God. While God does not expect the same things *from* each of us, God does have expectations *for* each of us. Our abilities, strengths, and resources are all different. But God holds each of us accountable for what we have, what we know, and whom we know.

As a teacher, I have a responsibility to help my students to recognize the gifts that are within them. Unfortunately, I am probably guilty of playing favorites. In our schools and in our churches, we may err by encouraging people with certain gifts while ignoring others. Often in our churches we praise and support the young person who has been called as a medical missionary or pastor but fail to support the young person who has been called to teach in the local school or to work as an engineer in the local factory. No matter what the gift, they all must be recognized and nurtured.

Very early in life, we begin to see how we measure up when it comes to the gift department. The concepts of superiority and inferiority become apparent at a very young age. I have two friends who each have a daughter in the first grade. These two 6-year-olds happen to be in the same class at school, and they have known each other all of their short lives. Jessica is an excellent reader, probably reading on about a fifth-grade level. It's actually pretty scary how advanced this child is in terms of language and reading. Lately her friend and classmate, Emily, has been coming home from school quite discouraged. Now Emily is very bright and is an excellent student, but she tells her mom, "It's not fair. Jessica knows every word. Why can't I read like she can?" And little does she know that Jessica is frustrated about a similar feeling of inferiority. You see, Emily is quite a dancer. Jessica and Emily are in the same dance class, and Jessica comes home from practice discouraged that she cannot learn the moves as quickly and perform them as well as Emily can. Fortunately, Jessica and Emily have very supportive parents who are helping them to see that we all have different gifts, and they are helping these two little girls to look for the important gifts within them. God does not see us in terms of superiority and inferiority. God bestows different gifts in varying amounts and wants us to appreciate and help nurture the potential we see in each other, not in competition but in a spirit of cooperation.

As in any case of cooperative effort, the individuals who have united toward a common goal should exhibit genuine love, affection, and honor toward one another. Read Romans 12:9–10. Practicing this call to walk in love within the community prepares the way for us to walk in the same spirit of love with those outside the community of faith.[9] The word "*love* (v.10) is *philostorgos*, a combination of *storge* and *philia*, of mother love and brother love."[10] This is an all-encompassing love. This love creates the base upon which we can relate to the entire community.

If I may go back to the example of Jessica and Emily for a minute, let's look at the difference between personal bests and all-out competition. Many Americans are obsessed with competition, with beating the other team or the other player. We use violent words like *slaughter, annihilate,* and *kill* to describe what we want to do to the other team. Unlike Jessica and Emily's desire to be the best they can be, in some cases we want to exercise our superiority at someone else's expense, to be better than they are. Often parents are guiltier of this than their children. Parents, sometimes desiring to live vicariously through their children, make idiots of themselves when an umpire makes a questionable call against their child or their child's team. The children who may be perfectly all right with the call are often embarrassed at their parents' reactions. No doubt, the example these zealous parents set has ramifications that we may not even realize. Imagine what sportsmanship would look like if we exercised Paul's words in 12:10 (NRSV), "Love one another with mutual affection; outdo one another in showing honor." Love wastefully, not knowing how that love will be received.

The 25th high school reunion that I mentioned earlier was quite illuminating to me in many ways. Jeffrey Davis, whose name incidentally bears a striking resemblance to the president of the Confederacy, was and is the president of our senior class. After our dinner of barbeque, rice, hash, and all the fixings, he humbly told us of a chance he had taken a few months before the reunion. I am ashamed to admit that for 25 years, our white classmates had had reunions separate from the black graduates of our class. I know it may be hard to believe that this kind of segregation was still being practiced after so many years. Jeffrey decided to end this outrage. When the black graduates had their reunion, Jeffrey showed up at the party and was the only white person in the room. He told us that he was treated like a king, even receiving the award for something like "best white boy dancer." Jeffrey then proceeded to invite our black classmates to the white students' reunion. At this reunion, after about an hour or so, two of our black classmates dropped by, and then several more came. After a wonderful time of catching up, Joyce, one of our black classmates, went to the microphone and said, "This has been a wonderful occasion. It's time we ended this separation. You all are invited to a party that we will be having over the holidays." We must honor each other and love wastefully because this is what is good, the right thing to do, even if it does take 25 years to happen.

Questions for personal reflection (vv. 6–10)

1. How can we help recognize and nurture the gifts that are within those people in our lives?
2. How can you give honor and show God's love in ways that may be difficult?
3. How do others in your home and community show honor and God's love to you?

Gospel responsibility to act and to minister

If our service within the kingdom of God is based on participation in the community, as we love others in the gift of grace, then we are prepared to act in a manner that demonstrates our spiritual commitment. As we will see throughout the remainder of this chapter of Romans, we have a responsibility to lend a hand to our friends, our associates, and even our enemies. In Romans 12:11–12, Paul cites the aspects of zeal we can have, as we are aglow with the Spirit, hopeful, patient, and constantly in prayer, which is necessary for faithful service. This prayer can help us especially in terms of our motives for service.

Paul's description of the Christian faith in Romans 12:1–12 then makes the natural move in verses 13–17 to the tangible acts of service which will result from a *faith* commitment. As Christians, we respond to the needs of those around us in spiritual as well as tangible ways. Responding to the needs of the saints implies that we are living in community with others and aware of their needs. Our individual gifts offer the necessary resources for meeting some of these needs, and our love for others should motivate us to approach others in an attitude of hospitality and service. Remembering at all times that our love is based on the grace of God, the only appropriate response to others is one of service and love. Love wastefully? Love is never wasted on anyone, and we should do it abundantly with abandon.

With so much to be done in the world to alleviate poverty, pain, and suffering we might be tempted to throw up our hands and ask, "What can I, one person, do to help, and how will what I do matter in the broad scheme of things?" While I cannot remember all of the details, I recall bits and pieces of a story that might help answer this question. As the story goes, at high tide each day, thousands of gasping starfish wash ashore on a particular beach. Unable to make it back to the ocean when the tide waters recede, these helpless creatures die untimely deaths in the hot sun because of their inability to crawl back to their ocean home. At that time of day, some entrepreneurial souls take advantage of the plight of these little victims. With buckets and bags in hand, these enterprising people gather the starfish to dry them and sell them to tourists wanting to preserve a portion of their beach vacations. Besides, the poor, suffocating creatures would just die anyway, right?

One day one of these gatherers spots a woman wildly and quickly picking up living starfish one by one, then flinging the weakened animals softly into the ocean. The gatherer approaches the woman and asks, "What are you doing?" The woman replies, "I'm saving them." Perplexed, the gatherer says, "But there are so many. How can you save them all? What difference can your efforts make?" At that moment the woman gently picks up a starfish clinging to the drying sand and hurls it into the water. "It makes a difference to that one."[11] Practice a random act of kindness to improve just one person's quality of life, even slightly, even for a day, even for a moment.

Sometimes we fail to love and make a difference because we are so obsessed with ourselves. Verse 16 is a reminder to all of us who as adolescents enjoyed being seen in good company. Somehow, if we hung out with the upper crust, we got the impression that not only might some of it rub off on us but also that people observing our rich company would think more highly of us. This consensual validation would give us higher self-esteem, even if we didn't deserve it. That's why some of us still enjoy having our pictures taken with famous people to be able to say, "Look at me and my company." Believe me; I am quite guilty of this sometimes petty attitude of trying to convince other people that I am better and smarter and more successful than I really am. But Paul gives us an earful here by saying, Don't be so haughty. Instead he tells us to associate with the lowly, the people who do not get a lot of positive publicity.

Jesus certainly was a good example to us here. He associated with tax collectors, women of ill repute, and lowly disciples who were simple fishermen and not very influential. Nakia, our precocious adolescent friend, says, "That was easy for Him. He was the greatest person to ever live, and He didn't need to impress anybody. I like to be seen with the movers and the shakers in my school. I know that is wrong of me, but I'm still working on my image." Like Nakia, many of us have uncertainty about our images and are trying to gain favor. I am reminded here of the politician who takes advantage of every photo opportunity that will make him or her look better in the voters' eyes. Many of them *will* seek the company of the lowly if cameras are around and if they want to be seen as champions of the poor. But when the cameras leave the impoverished areas, often these politicians follow them. It's important to keep in mind here that we are also guilty of pointing out the faults of politicians in much the same way that the people of Jesus' day pigeonholed tax collectors. We will see more on this later.

Recently one of my students received an invitation to have lunch at a local restaurant with two gay men who were "out" in our community, one of whom has AIDS. Upon hearing of his lunch engagement, an acquaintance said to Greg, "Aren't you afraid if you're seen having a meal with them that other people will think you are condoning their behavior and will possibly think you're gay too?" While I would hardly call these two gay men "lowly," many people in my community would categorize them as such, particularly the man who has AIDS. What do you think Paul would have said about this situation, especially given his words in Romans 1? What do you think Jesus would say?

Questions for personal reflection (vv. 11-17)

1. Ask God to enlarge your focus. List things God urges you to do.
2. Whom do you know who exemplifies service and love?
3. How can you improve someone's quality of life, even slightly, even for a day, even for a moment?
4. Who are the "lowly" people in your community with whom Paul instructs us to associate?

Called to be peacemakers

When we think of peacemaking, the Middle East, Bosnia, and other parts of the world often come to mind. Certainly these areas are in dire need of peace and our prayers and support go out to them. Recognizing that Christians do not have control over all their circumstances, Paul reminds us in Romans 12:18–21 that our calling in a world of strife is to be people of peace. As peacemakers, we should always respond peaceably, strive for justice, and act justly. And here, we're not just talking about in the Middle East or Bosnia.

I have an associate with whom I have little theological commonality. In fact, his view of Scripture, especially Paul's writings, and mine are nearly total opposites. And, of course, I feel my opinions are always right, and his never are! Often I find myself wanting to lash out at him to get him to see things my way; but whenever I am in his presence, his kindness overwhelms me to the point that my anger and difference dissolve and my demeanor changes. He is a peacemaker and has been a tremendous faith influence in my life; and through his pleasant disposition, he turns our differences to friendship. While my associate is not really my enemy and in no way is he evil, this relationship helps me understand what Paul is saying in verse 20 concerning our enemies.

In this verse, Paul is quoting Proverbs 25:22, which has often been misunderstood in terms of our motives for befriending our enemies. Paul is not saying that this is how we get back at our enemies. He is saying that kindness gets the enemy to turn from wrath to friendship, from hate to love, from strife to peace. This is much the same way God deals with us when we are rebellious and act in ungodly ways.[12] As we encounter strife, we have a responsibility to respond with the goodness that represents the grace God has offered us. In this way others will be able to see the kingdom of God lived out in their midst.

As mentioned at the beginning of this chapter, the days of Ozzie and Harriet are gone, and no longer do we live in homogeneous communities where everyone looks alike and believes the same thing. Those who love Christ have a gospel responsibility to live peaceably with all and to love and honor our friends and even those we might consider our enemies. In so doing maybe we *will* improve someone's quality of life, even slightly, even for a day, even for a moment.

Questions for personal reflection (vv. 18–21)

1. How can you be a peacemaker this week?
2. Name one situation where there is no peace and list steps you can take to reduce friction, stress, or problems.

[1]Robert Wuthnow, *After Heaven: Spirituality in America Since the 1950's* (Los Angeles: University of California Press, 1998).
[2]Wade Clark Roof, *A Generation of Seekers* (San Francisco: Harper San Francisco, 1993), 70, quoted in Richard Cimino and Don Lattin, *Shopping for Faith: American Religion in the New Millennium* (San Francisco: Jossey-Bass Publishers, 1998), 12–13.
[3]Clifton J. Allen, ed., *The Broadman Bible Commentary* (Nashville: Broadman Press, 1970), 10:248.
[4]Franz J. Leenhardt, *The Epistle to the Romans*, quoted in Allen, *Broadman Bible Commentary*, 10:249.
[5]Clarence Jordan, *The Cotton Patch Version of Paul's Epistles* (New York: Association Press, 1968), 38.
[6]Allen, *Broadman Bible Commentary*, 10:251.
[7]Barbara Kingsolver, *The Bean Trees* (New York: Harpercollins, 1988), 107–8.
[8]Allen, *Broadman Bible Commentary*, 10:251.
[9]Ibid., 252.
[10]Ibid., 253.
[11]Based on Loren C. Eiseley, *The Star Thrower* (New York: Harcourt Brace, 1979).
[12]Paul J. Achtemeier, *Romans: Interpretation: A Bible Commentary for Teaching and Preaching* (Louisville, KY: John Knox Press, 1985), 202.

10

The Urgency of Gospel Responsibility

Romans 13–14

A couple in my town was convinced that at the stroke of midnight on December 31, 1999, Jesus was coming again. Thinking no future was in store for them on this earth, they sold their house, cashed in all their stocks and CDs, took all the money, and went around the world twice over a 3-year period spending their last red cent. I sincerely hope they had a great trip.

While Paul's thoughts were not this drastic, the 13th and 14th chapters of Romans have the undercurrent of Paul's belief that the return of Christ was imminent. You see this in many of his writings. This belief led him to his view of governmental authority, responsible financial living, living as a Christian in nonjudgmental ways, and developing Christian convictions that will sustain and support Christian faith.

Accountable to civil rule

"'Render therefore to Caesar the things which are Caesar's, and to God the things that are God's'" (Matt. 22:21 NKJV). Jesus spoke these words when asked if it were lawful to pay taxes to the emperor or not. Jesus asked for a coin (which I'm sure He gave back!) and asked, "'Whose image and inscription is this?'" (Matt. 22:20 NKJV). The answer was clear.

A visiting professor at my college pointed out in a recent lecture that American government bears a striking resemblance to Roman government. Look at our coins and the images of the presidents on them. Roman coins looked the same with the emperors' heads in profile. Look at the inscription over the head of the eagle on the flip side of a quarter. It says the same thing as Roman coins and is written in the language of ancient Rome, Latin. Even the eagle is the same symbol the Romans used. As this lecturer pointed out, in many ways Americans think they are Romans.

Like those Romans, we all must function in a world that is governed by official authorities and rules. If we think about it, we would probably agree that most of us function better within a system of responsibility and accountability. Within societies, families, even friendships, there are rules, both written and unwritten. When we fail to follow the rules, things are often chaotic and we suffer the consequences. Families, societies, governments, even friendships all work best when we follow certain guidelines. No doubt, at times we become frustrated with some of the rules, particularly if our political party is not in the majority when the rules or laws are made. Reconciling these authority figures, rules, and civil obligations with the call to be Christians can be a difficult task. The same challenge was true when Paul wrote his letter to the Romans.

The centralized government in Rome offered many advantages to its citizens and travelers, but at the same time it was not a guaranteed supporter of the Christian faith. Depending on the particular person in power, the Roman government was not always friendly toward Christianity, and certainly in the times after Paul wrote this letter, the government often acted as an enemy toward Christianity.

Opportunities for confusion and conflict between loyalties for Christian citizens are frequent, but when governmental authority acts on the "authority" of God, Paul suggests that the role of the Christian citizen becomes a little easier to live out. As ordained by God, he says authorities act as both extensions of God's goodness and God's judgment.

I don't think I ever correctly learned the rule about four-way stops. I hate to see one because invariably I sit there waiting my turn until somebody helpfully blows a horn. Then I wonder what would happen if everybody were as ignorant of the law as I am in this situation. I guess we'd all still be sitting at the corner waiting for someone to blow the horn. For Paul the issue is not one of just civil obedience but also one of understanding the role of social institutions in maintaining the social order. Without this respect for the social order, chaos becomes a real threat, and it would have greater ramifications than four stopped cars at an intersection.

Read Romans 13:1–5. We should not interpret *obey* or *be subject to* (NRSV) in verse 1 as mindless servitude. Rather the term implies mutual respect and submission as unto a sister or brother, much the same way as we see in Ephesians 5:21. Christians should live out their submission not out of a sense of fear of the power which authority holds but out of a sense of freedom and love for Christ.

I recently heard a news report of a man who was arrested after running from a police officer. The man had done absolutely nothing; but when the officer approached him, he ran. If I had been the officer, I too would have been suspicious and would probably have begun pursuit. While I do not know the whole story, I would think the man had no need to feel guilty just because he saw an authority of the law. If we are behaving, there is no need of fear as Paul says in verses 3–5.

Questions for personal reflection

1. How do you view the federal government? Your state government? Your local government?
2. What do you do to follow Paul's advice about government?

Responsible for taxes and debts

That fear of authority sometimes comes when we hear the words *tax audit* or *creditors*. Read Romans 13:6–8. Christian participation in society involves fulfilling financial obligations, including those demanded by the state such as taxes. Within this context, Paul reminds us that the Christian's place is to honor all obligations promptly and to avoid debts, except the debt of love. The love that we owe to others can never be completely paid, so it is the one legitimate debt.

I received my W-2 form from the college the same day I began working on this section. That helped put verses 6–7 in perspective! Without getting too political with the debates over a flat tax, wasteful spending, or reducing taxes or raising them, let me simply say that revenue is necessary to pay for many things our country needs such as roads and schools. About 10 years ago, one of my students challenged this whole notion and responded in a drastic way. She and her family believed that the government was not spending federal and state revenue wisely. Believing that too much money was being spent on the military and welfare, this family decided to prorate their taxes according to the initiatives and programs they supported. They subtracted the percentages spent on the programs with which they were in conflict and sent in an amount much less than the tax schedule specified. I don't know if they ever got caught; but I do know that if every taxpayer did this, our country would be in trouble, not to mention the errant taxpayers. As Paul says, we have an obligation to "pay . . . taxes to whom taxes are due" (v. 7). April 15 is inevitable, like it or not.

Money is a difficult subject for many people, particularly for those of us who owe a lot of it. The subject of debt is one that spreads fear in the hearts of college students who have borrowed tens of thousands of dollars to finance their education. While they spend much of the money on room and board, books, and legitimate software, many students often splurge a bit too much sometimes indulging in expensive meals, pricey concerts, designer clothes, and even new cars. Not only do some max out their loans, they also make the mistake of being enticed by those little rectangular pieces of plastic. One of my students is at her limit on four different credit cards and wonders how she will ever pay them off along with her student loans.

These students are not alone in their difficult plight to pay off their debts. Much like the couple described at the beginning of this chapter, we sometimes spend as if there is no tomorrow. The minimum amount due on those cards each month is deceiving, especially with double-digit interest rates. But as Paul says in verse 8, we have a responsibility to pay our debts, and we also have a responsibility to control our spending.

Questions for personal reflection (13:6–8)

1. From your perspective, how might tax law be changed to better serve God and country?
2. Pray about your debts. What does the Holy Spirit lead you to do about any charge accounts, credit cards, or debts?

Accountable for just living

We cannot repay the debt of love we owe, and we cannot spend too much love. While fulfillment of the debt of love toward those around us is a perpetual one as we saw in verse 8, fulfillment of the commandments also demands our attention. Beginning in Romans 13:9, Paul offers a commonly used summary of the Old Testament commandments by citing Exodus 20:13–17. The first part of verse 9 then gives us a portion of those things from which we should refrain. Verse 9 ends with the words of Jesus recorded in Matthew 22:39, Mark 12:31, and Luke 10:27, first cited in Leviticus 19:18. Here we see that loving our neighbor as we love ourselves sums up all of the commandments.

Remember here that Jesus explained what He meant by neighbor by telling the parable of the good Samaritan in Luke 10. No doubt our notion of neighbor must be quite inclusive, not just the Taylors and the Lowns next door but including the prisoners and the people who do us harm. Notice that verse 10 reminds us that love, not obedience, is the fulfillment of the law explained in these verses. Love goes far beyond legal obligations and rules. Perhaps one of the most beautiful passages of Scripture written by Paul, 1 Corinthians 13, expands on this notion comparing love to faith and hope and concludes that love is the greatest gift we can receive or give. And what a wonderful gift it is! Thanks be to God!

Questions for personal reflection (13:9–10)

1. How might you broaden your definition of neighbor?
2. How do you show your debt of love to your family? to fellow Christians? to your community?

Gospel responsibility in an urgent age

"It's about time we took Jesus seriously." The time for acting on these Christian convictions is now. As George Albert Coe said decades ago, it's time to quit paying lip service and get on with our gospel responsibility. Read Romans 13:11. Paul uses the image of day and night to convey the concepts of action and waiting. For Paul, the time of waiting is over and the time for moral action has come. As Clarence Jordan states the urgency of time, "Let's take off our pajamas and put on our work clothes."[1] Compare Jordan's words to those in verse 12.

One way that Christians should prepare themselves for the day at hand is through a life that is honorable to Christ. Read carefully Romans 13:13–14, to see how Paul explains this idea. In light of the return of Christ and the coming age, this is no time to be honoring the flesh. Paul lists behavior that reflects conduct not of Christ: reveling and drunkenness (lack of moral restraint), debauchery and licentiousness (shameless immorality), and quarreling and jealousy (antisocial behavior and envy). Most of these behaviors have to do with a lack of self-control. Aristotle would call this virtue temperance. Daniel Goleman sees self-control as being a major characteristic in what he calls EQ, or emotional intelligence.[2] Those who have high emotional intelligence exercise temperance or control over the impulses to do those things listed above as well as many things not included in these verses.

Even if we think we have successfully refrained from some of the behavior on this list, we must keep in mind that the list goes on and on. I know what I do that is not Christlike, and I must refrain. I must try to improve my EQ by seeking to emulate Christ. Even though Christ's coming was not as imminent as Paul thought, we must take Jesus seriously now.

Responsible to refrain from judgment

One of my seminary professors told the class of a time that he and his wife had dinner with a couple while visiting in Germany. All through the meal, the two wives glared at each other. The husbands did not have a clue what the problem was. Later that night, the two men asked their wives why they were less than cordial toward each other. The issue was judgment of the other for what each considered an awful practice. The American woman glared at the German woman because she was serving beer as an option during the meal. The German woman glared at the American woman because she was wearing makeup. We are all probably guilty on some level of judging.

When my students sometimes ask me if I think a certain person or group of people will be ultimately punished for their behavior, my response is, "I don't get paid to think on that level. That judgment is not up to me." Then they want to know if certain Old Testament prohibitions are still operative and what their responsibility is to refrain from behaviors that may cause their friends to stumble. Paul speaks to many of these questions in chapter 14 of Romans.

Here Paul uses the examples of dietary laws and observances of holy days to demonstrate the acceptance Christians should display. Under consideration here is the tension that had erupted between those "weak in faith" and those "strong in faith." Read Romans 14:1–10 and see how many ways Paul compares the two lifestyles.

Those weak in faith were those who held more closely to certain customs and laws. The strong in faith were those who had sufficient knowledge to understand that Christian liberty did not require such regulation. The strong did not need the restrictions that the weak imposed on themselves and these two groups were threatening the unity of the Christian community in Rome. Jewish law did not forbid the eating of meat or the drinking of wine, and neither did Paul. He neither sided with nor condemned the weak or the strong, and his advice to both groups was the same: "Respect the convictions of the other group."[3] Tolerance is a key issue here. Paul hoped to bring the majority and minority factions into fellowship and remind each that the role of judge is God's alone. We are not paid to think on that level.

Arrogance and self-righteousness make us do stupid things. Rather than our motives being to honor God, we do things to bring honor to ourselves. We usually think we know best and we think our way is the right way. Our opinions of certain customs are often based not on laws or commandments but instead on simple preferences or societal customs. A big difference exists between values and virtues.

Hannah had observed the Lord's Supper only a time or two in her young life at my church. Hannah watched intently as the little pieces of bread were passed on a silver tray, and she carefully selected a perfect piece. Savoring every morsel, she slowly swallowed the body of Christ. As the juice was coming her way, she looked up at the man sitting next to her and said, "Do we get cheese with this?"

Later Hannah's mother told me that she had to limit her little girl's lactose intake, and every chance she got, Hannah looked for cheese. She had a weakness for this delicacy that she was forbidden to eat. This had nothing to do with any doctrine or law or virtue, but only with a preference for a food she valued very much.

Values are not always good and, again, have more to do with preferences. Virtues, however, are always desirable. Aristotle hailed four virtues as being of utmost importance: prudence (or practical wisdom), fortitude (or strength of mind and perseverance in the face of adversity), temperance (or self-discipline that we mentioned earlier), and justice (or fairness). Many of these are reflected in these words of Paul. Of course faith, hope, and love mentioned in 1 Corinthians 13 along with many of the virtues listed in Matthew 5 such as meekness or humility, mercy, and peacemaking round out this list. All of these are virtues that are qualities of character involved in doing the right thing, doing the Christlike thing. Values are a different story.

Are some values bad? Of course they are. I might value certain movies that some would consider bad. I might value hoarding wealth (or greed). I might value certain art that critics would call bad. Again, these values have to do with mere preferences that may or may not be good. We must take care to make sure that we do not confuse values with virtues, especially when it comes to the debate over the customs mentioned earlier and the ones that we will see subsequently in this 14th chapter of Romans. Virtues are not up for grabs. Some values are.

Questions for personal reflection (vv. 14:1–10)

1. Name some differences of values among people you know.
2. Against which differences or values are you prejudiced?
3. In which areas do you find that you judge unfairly?

Responsible to confess Jesus as Lord

Paul splices the concepts of God alone as judge together with a statement of the lordship of Christ. Romans 14:11 is a pivotal verse to focus the thoughts of all those in the church in Rome on Jesus Christ. Our petty differences will find no validity in light of the lordship of Christ that will be proclaimed at the final judgment. Paul's words here remind us that our calling is to proclaim and serve the cause of Christ in all our actions.

Responsible to set a good example

To think that I might be an example is a humbling thought and often gets in the way of acting on my selfish, worldly impulses. I don't always want to acknowledge that I may be being a faith influence for someone unknowingly. Whether we are responding to a cashier at the grocery store or to those solicitation phone callers during dinner, our behavior should reflect our understanding of the call of Christ. In this call is great freedom and liberty that is to be exercised through love. Read in Romans 14:12–18 how Paul proposes we should live. The focus of our actions, while couched in terms of liberty and love, should always actively contribute to the work of God. This may mean that in some circumstances we act in deference to others and choose not to exercise the complete extent of our freedom. Common courtesy and, again, respect must often win out over what we see as our right or privilege.

Questions for personal reflection (14:12–18)

1. Explain Paul's view of freedom and tolerance. How far does this issue of tolerance go?
2. How much responsibility do we have to others to exercise restraint in situations that are simply preferences?

Called to edify others

While many actions may be allowable for us in the freedom which salvation affords, our primary concern should always be love and concern for our fellow human beings, both Christians and those who do not profess Christ. In Romans 14:19–21 Paul refers to some of the social customs of his day, such as eating meat and drinking wine, over which first-century Christians disagreed. While the simple acts of eating or drinking are not indicative of our Christian commitment, our attention to the spiritual growth of others is an act of faith. There, we may need to avoid certain behavior out of concern for another's position in the faith. Consider the following example.

Our young friend Nakia, 14, had some questions about this passage, particularly in light of a recent confrontation by a friend. Liz learned through a friend of a friend that Nakia's mother sometimes served wine with dinner when she entertained guests. Liz said, "I heard your mother is a wine drinker. Doesn't she know that Christians should not do that?"

Nakia said, "How do you know that it is wrong?"

"Because the Bible teaches us that in Leviticus 10:9, 1 Timothy 3:8, and a bunch of other places in both the Old and New Testaments," replied Liz.

Nakia responded, "What do you think happened at the wedding at Cana in John 2 when Jesus turned the water into wine?"

"Well, that was because the water was bad and wine was all they had to drink," said Liz.

"Don't you think if Jesus could turn water into wine, that He could have turned bad water into good water? And besides, we are not talking about a bottle or two. Just look at verse 6 in John chapter 2."

Nakia continued, "Jesus made six jars of wine each holding 20 or 30 gallons. That's 120 to 180 gallons. I'd say that was quite a party, especially considering that they had already run out of wine one time."

Nakia concluded by saying, "If Jesus thought it was OK, then my mom shouldn't be judged for serving a glass here and there."

Liz responded, "Well, if some people *think* it's wrong for them, then it *is* wrong for them. Just look at Romans 14:14."

Still defending her mother, Nakia said, "My mama serves wine only when she knows that people are OK with it. She would never offer wine to an alcoholic or to someone who thinks it's wrong."

This discussion may extend to our vegetarian friends. Vegetarianism for the sake of the animal is not the issue in these passages but may be an issue among many people today. I have some friends who do not eat meat because they believe it is wrong to kill another animal to use for food when there are so many other options. One of my friends bases her conviction on an early adolescent experience; and while I do not fully understand her feelings, I must respect them. When she comes to my home as a dinner guest, if I serve meat at all, it is merely an option. She never takes a self-righteous stance here; and often when I am in her home, she will make an extra effort to serve a dish with meat for those who prefer it. While she certainly respects my preference, I must genuinely respect her conviction; and, in all reality, her diet is actually much healthier than mine.

In today's society, eating, drinking, and the observance of holy days may not be our primary points of difference in expressing our Christian faith, but the principle of striving toward Christian unity remains constant. The goal is for all Christians to work together to bring about the peace of the kingdom of God. Toward this goal, differences in practice, lifestyle, and custom can become trivial. This may be a question of values or preferences rather than virtues or commands. Either way, common courtesy and respect go a long way in preserving friendships and in establishing peaceable relations.

Responsible to live with assurance

Living with an "assurance as to the leading of the Spirit" is a theme Paul uses in Romans 14:22–23.[4] Faith is a personal expression of belief and commitment. Motive is key here. Actions that express our faith can retain their meaning only if they are the sincere result of genuine belief. We are accountable to God alone for our convictions.

In this passage, Paul seeks to explain the importance of achieving inner peace and convictions that are the consequences of a thoughtful and personal faith. To have doubts is not bad; but as Clarence Jordan says, one who lacks conviction and straddles the fence "is in a bad way."[5] In these days of paranoia and what Achtemeier calls this "me first" generation,[6] we must not do as the couple at the beginning of this chapter did and cash in everything for one last fling that is fleeting. We must seek the lasting inner peace that God has to offer through Jesus Christ for ourselves and for our neighbors.

Questions for personal reflection (vv. 19–21)

1. Do you observe certain rules about eating and drinking? Why?
2. How do you tell the difference between preferences and God-given mandates? Is this relatively easy for you?
3. When is doubting helpful and a point of growth in your life?

[1]Clarence Jordan, *The Cotton Patch Version of Paul's Epistles* (New York: Association Press, 1968), 40.

[2]Daniel Goleman, *Emotional Intelligence: Why It Can Matter More Than IQ* (New York: Bantam Books, 1995), 194.

[3]Paul J. Achtemeier, *Romans,* vol. in *Interpretation: A Bible Commentary for Teaching and Preaching* (Louisville, KY: John Knox Press, 1985), 216.

[4]George Arthur Buttrick, ed., *The Interpreter's Bible* (Nashville: Abingdon Press, 1978), 9:631.

[5]Jordan, *Cotton Patch Version,* 42.

[6]Achtemeier, *Romans,* 222.

11

Gospel Responsibility to Spread the Love of God to All Nations

Romans 15

Nakia asks, "Why should I have to watch everything that I do just because it might offend other people? Isn't that their problem? Where does my freedom end and their interests start?" Nakia's questions are good ones, ones that we often ask given the differences between values and virtues discussed previously. If an act or a desire has more to do with one's preference than with law, how considerate do we need to be of others' feelings and weaknesses?

Responsible to consider others and to live righteously in our neighborhoods

"Christian maturity is our ability to subordinate our own desires and our own preferences to the actual necessities of those who are weaker than we are."[1] These words capture the essence of Paul's message to the Christians at Rome. In chapter 14, he refers to some of the ways Christians can encourage and edify one another. Romans 15 directly addresses the ways Christians can show mutual respect, concern, and love for all; and while Romans 14 was directed to both the strong and the weak, Paul specifically speaks to the strong in the first part of chapter 15. "We who are strong ought to put up with the failings of the weak" (v. 1 NRSV). Those who are weak should receive more of the benefit of the doubt. Paul uses the word *strong* in Romans 15:1 to convey the concepts of freedom, maturity, and power. These characteristics are the result of the foundation of our faith in Christ, not the result of any strength we can claim as our own. Just as Christ imposed self-limitation on Himself for the sake of others, so should strong Christians.

If these traits in us are consistent and trustworthy, then our personalities must also be genuine. As Karl Barth says, the exhortation to "bear the infirmities of the weak"[2] does not simply mean to overlook the infirmities of the weak or to patronize them, but actually means "being weak with the weak,"[3] being weak for the good of others and for the sake of others.

Read carefully Romans 15:2–4 (NRSV). When Paul reminds us that "each of us must please our neighbor," does it remind you that all the people you know deserve your care and respect? What about those people you do not know? We should not interpret the word *pleasing* as "making others happy." The New Testament is not based on such superficial principles. Rather the call is to treat others with respect and always to keep the best interests of others in mind without any rivalry or superiority. Quoting Psalm 69:9 in verse 3 and pointing to Old Testament Scripture in verse 4, Paul reminds us also that these Old Testament Scriptures were written for our instruction and were not intended only for the times in which they were written.

As he has said before, Paul is telling us to avoid our "me first" tendencies. Clarence Jordan's special, "tell it like it is" manner puts verse 3 in these words: "For

Christ didn't put his interests first, but he did as the Scripture says: 'The spit of those spitting at you hit me.'"[4] Stepping into the line of fire for the sake of someone else involves self-sacrifice beyond the beneficence of most of us. But sometimes the love of God shines through us in amazing ways.

Riley was the 6-year-old brother of Ryan who was 8. When Ryan was diagnosed with a fatal kidney disease, one of his kidneys had to be removed. The family was told that in order for Ryan to stand a chance at survival, he would need a kidney transplant. Knowing the difficulty of matching a donor outside the family, tests were done to seek a familial donor. Little Riley was a nearly perfect match. His parents explained to him that in order for Ryan to live, the doctors would need to take a kidney from Riley to place in Ryan's weak body. Riley responded, "I know Ryan needs to live. He is so sick. I will give him my kidney." As the day for the transplant approached, both brothers were talking about the surgery on their way to a doctor's appointment. Ryan thanked his brother for being so brave to give up a kidney so that he could live. Not understanding the exact procedure, little brother Riley, the donor, asked his parents in the front seat, "So will I die before Ryan gets the kidney or after they put it in him?" Riley believed that he was giving up his life, not just his kidney for his brother. These redemptive glimpses of humanity and sacrifice among us remind us of Christ's ultimate sacrifice for all His siblings. While most of us will not be called on to give this much of ourselves, how much are we willing to give? How much are we willing to bear the infirmities of the weak?

Questions for personal reflection (15:1–4)

1. How do you bear the burdens of the weak?
2. Ask the Holy Spirit to show you what Romans 15 should mean in your interpersonal relationships.
3. Name four people who may think you feel superior to them. How can you change the situation?

Called to like-mindedness

One of the results of the respect and love we show for others should be the harmony in which we live. Read Romans 15:5–6. Paul proposes that harmony of thought leads to harmony of life. The standard by which this "likeness" is measured is Christ.

My college is a small, fairly homogeneous community where all staff and faculty and nearly every student is a Christian. Despite this unity in Christ, we have many differences of opinion on certain issues such as gun control, homosexuality, abortion, and welfare. For example, my colleague Bill and I are on opposite ends of the political spectrum on most issues. But we are good friends and actually enjoy hearing each other's take on various topics. After each discussion, I come away with a new appreciation of him and his view.

At times, debates among people at my college get quite lively when these issues arise. But in most cases, a spirit of civility and respect comes through as we seek to be like-minded at least in our processing of the issues. Diversity of opinion is good and should not be considered a detriment to the health of a college, a church, a family, or any organization. It has been said that when we all think alike, nobody thinks much. "Good harmony is tension in balance."[5] Paul is not saying in verses 5 and 6 that we cannot have differences of opinion, but he is saying that in the midst of those differences, we must seek charity and harmony. Respect is a key issue here.

Christ is the Maestro Who conducts the symphony made up of many different instruments each playing in harmony for His glory. The squawk of the oboe is needed just as the hum of the violin is. Such harmony is a product of a blending of the sounds of the weaker instruments with those of the strong, all made possible by the overwhelming love of God.

Just as our individual actions should demonstrate the glory of God and Christ, God also expects that our corporate actions should be unified in their direction and purpose. This like-mindedness will also serve as the foundation for the Christian community. As Romans 15:7 states, in the *accepting* of others, we will live out the call to serve and live and echo the welcome that has been extended to us by Christ.

As I sit writing this in my back room in the mountains of North Carolina, snow is falling heavily but gently, covering my deck with a blanket of immaculate whiteness. Before the snow came, the deck was littered with debris from trees all around my house brought there by a powerful windstorm the day before. A diversity of remnants of nature, sticks, leaves, and bark, lay scattered on the rough wooden floor. Now I can no longer see that debris. The deck is spotless and pure, made clean by the downy flakes. Just as the snow covers the litter of nature, Christ covers us in every sense of the word, all of us in all our diversity.

Questions for personal reflection (vv. 5–6)

1. Are you in harmony with all people? Your family? Your neighbors? Fellow church members? Fellow workers? Other races? Other cultures?

2. What are some steps you can take to live more harmoniously with others?

Responsible to welcome all

Southerners have been notorious for sometimes having difficulty welcoming "Yankees" into their communities. "You must not be from here" is a phrase often used to indicate that you're real different from us, you don't understand the way things operate here, and you just might not fit in. Even after a Yankee family has lived in a southern community for a while and had a baby or two, even the children may not be fully welcomed. A proud southerner once said, "Just 'cause the cat has kittens in the oven, it don't make 'em biscuits." Old prejudices die hard, but we are responsible to welcome all.

Paul now brings the description of Christian community full circle. Once again admonishing us to live together, Paul addresses the issue of exclusivism and nationalism. Read Romans 15:7–8. Regardless of national origin, God calls all of us to live in the grace of Christ with mutual welcoming not only of Jew and Gentile but also Republican and Democrat, black and white, Yankee and Southerner, Cuban and American. God calls us to live in community with others and to share actively this hope through our praise and rejoicing that we see in Romans 15:9–10.

We tend to overuse the words *joy* and *peace*; our society undervalues their concepts. Notice that Romans 15:10–12 repeats the theme of joy. Joy and peace, in their fullest meaning, represent the absence of fear, bondage, guilt, and obligation. They can offer great redemptive value for us as we seek to live in harmony with those who at times try our peaceful natures and we theirs. Where verses 1–6 ended with a benediction, we see the same in verses 7–13. In a lovely way Paul says in verse 13

(NRSV), "May the God of hope fill you with all joy and peace in believing." And may we extend that joy and peace to everyone.

Questions for personal reflection (vv. 7–13)

1. Describe what you mean by peace.
2. What simple things give you joy and peace in your life? How has Christ given you joy and peace?
3. What is the Holy Spirit's role in your hope, as you understand the meaning of Romans 15:13?

Called to goodness through grace

"Well done, my good and faithful servant." These words are music to the ears of many of us. From the early days of check marks and gold stars, approval for a job well done and a life well lived affirm our desire and efforts to serve God. Compliments are the uplifts that often give us the strength to help us persevere. Paul gives such positive reinforcement to the church at Rome. "I myself feel confident about you, my brothers and sisters, that you yourselves are full of goodness," Paul says in verse 14 (NRSV). These must have been great words of encouragement to the Christians there. Paul comments on his knowledge of the manner in which the church at Rome has lived out goodness and just as importantly has taken responsibility for their own spiritual growth.

While Paul does have some words of edification to offer the church at Rome, he does not overlook their ability and history of edifying themselves. This is a model for Christians today. Our goodness and concern for spiritual growth should be apparent to all those who see us. Just as the church at Rome had a reputation for goodness and instruction, our reputations should reflect these characteristics in our own lives. Through actions and words, we demonstrate to the world what is valuable to us.

Questions for personal reflection (v. 14)

1. Exactly what is valuable to you?
2. How do you show it?
3. What are some specific ways you edify or build up both the Christians and the people you know who are not Christians?

Responsible to share the gospel message of hope

In recognizing that the church at Rome had ministered to its own needs, Paul sets the stage for the aspect of ministry for all Christians, beginning with Romans 15:15. While the word *servant* (or *minister*) in verse 16 could refer to civil as well as religious work, Barclay summarizes the use of the word in the New Testament as "offerings for public use."[6]

Paul also uses the word generally agreed to mean "to serve like a priest." With these two aspects, Paul's own example of ministry becomes clear. His ministry to the Gentile world demonstrates Christ as the source and sustainer, the gospel as the truth and hope for the world, and the Spirit as the enabler.

Our contemporary world may differ in many ways from the world in which Paul lived, but the basic need for people to share the gospel message of hope and salvation has not changed. The role of priest and minister belongs to each of us as we encounter the pain and hopelessness in our world. And each of us is uniquely gifted to offer to others what we have been so abundantly given.

Questions for personal reflection (vv. 15–16)

1. How do you give your life as an "offering for public use"?
2. How do you serve others and minister to their needs?

Called to power and to spread the gospel

As we will see in verses 22–33, Paul has a full travel agenda with three primary stops, in Rome, in Spain, and in Jerusalem. This is an ambitious itinerary, no doubt, one requiring support and resources. He is both grateful for and covets these in this letter to the Romans.

Paul is quick to give credit where credit is due. We see his humility in the midst of his achievement as Paul credits any influence or success his ministry may have had to the power of the Holy Spirit in verses 17–19. While these words are particularly significant for the itinerant type of ministry in which Paul operated, they are not any less important for all who participate in the ministry of Christ. The Holy Spirit often works through us even in spite of ourselves and our selfishness.

Read Romans 15:20–25. Believing the gospel message was valuable for all people, Paul was not content to stay in the comfort and security of places where the word of Christ had already been preached. He understood his work in the kingdom of God to extend into areas where no foundation for the gospel had yet been laid. This would, of course, mean that Paul would encounter hostility and difficulty.

Recently I heard a debate, and what a raucous debate it was, between two Christian leaders and two Jewish leaders. I was frankly a bit surprised that these four godly individuals could not control themselves better than they did. No doubt, each felt passionate about his position, but charity and humility were quite noticeable by their absence. The Christians voiced that they have been told to preach the gospel of Jesus Christ so that all have opportunity to hear of Christ's saving grace. The Jews responded that they had heard the message over and over again. The Christians added that not only must they hear the gospel but they must also understand it. The Jews, one of whom has a PhD in New Testament, said that they had read the New Testament over and over many times, had studied Christian commentary after Christian commentary, and had taken many classes taught by Christians. One of the Christians, not to be outdone, finally said in a loud and forceful voice, "Christ *commanded* us to go to all nations and teach them to observe all things He had commanded. We have no choice to do otherwise." Now getting quite agitated, the younger Jewish leader replied, "You have done your duty to us again and again. Now leave us alone."

How do you respond to this exchange of words? What would Jesus say? Do you believe we should never give up in our zeal to win others to Christ? What do you think of the approach of these two Christians?

In verse 20 we see that Paul saw himself as a planter. Clarence Jordan paraphrases Paul's words here: "I consider it a special privilege to tell the story where people never saw a live Christian before, lest I get credit for someone else's spadework."[7] Exposure to the gospel was key for Paul, even if the places he visited were less than hospitable. His enemies in Judea had already tried to kill him one time (2 Cor. 11:32–33; Acts 9:23–25), so Paul was asking for prayers for his safety.[8]

This look at Paul's work also points to the need for those who are willing to travel and speak the word of Christ. Paul's example demonstrates the necessity for those to come alongside and behind these preachers of the word and invest themselves in the long-term relationships through which growth and edification take place.

Questions for personal reflection

1. Why did Paul travel? What did he do in these places?
2. Where is God urging you to go? What is God urging you to do?

Gospel responsibility to support missions and to minister

Paul clearly understood the many ways fellow Christian believers throughout his travels supported his particular ministry. Read Romans 15:26–29. He specifically cites his gratitude for the monetary gifts that have been gathered as acts of service and love. These gifts are a gesture of unity and represent the love the saints have for the person and work of Christ, for the people of their world, and for Paul and his work.

The life and death of Mother Teresa have had a tremendous faith influence on me. Like those for whom Paul was grateful, many beneficent individuals made it possible for her to serve God in a mighty way. Teresa could have opted for a life that was much more safe and certainly more comfortable, but instead she chose to go where many fear to tread and have no desire to tread. Whether it was changing the soiled bed of a person with

AIDS or holding in her arms a dying, malnourished child, Teresa did it all, and she did it willingly.

I remember being affected greatly upon hearing of her death in 1997. Reports indicated that at the time of her death, all of her earthly possessions would have fit on a small table. While I can't recall exactly what was reported, I believe her possessions consisted of a wooden bucket, a rosary, a Bible, and three articles of clothing. She was often quoted as saying, "I do not care what you believe; I care about what you need." This, of course, does not mean that Teresa was indifferent about a person's faith. It means that she did not discriminate when it came to service. In an age in which consumerism has reached staggering heights, the faith of this unassuming, diminutive woman has influenced millions, calling us to gospel responsibility.

Four high school friends gathered together for lunch for the first time in more than 10 years. These women decided on one of the best restaurants in town where the menu was superb. After being seated at a table by the window, they began to peruse the elaborate menu offering exotic salads, exquisite entrées, and decadent desserts. When their meals arrived, a veritable plethora of delicacies was placed before them: roasted duck with an orange glaze, veal medallions, smoked salmon rubbed with herbs, marinated Portobello mushrooms, linguine with a basil and dried tomato cream sauce, garlic mashed potatoes sprinkled with three cheeses . . . the list went on an on. As the classmates began to enjoy their meals, one of the women looked out the window and noticed an older homeless woman practically standing on her head trying to retrieve some scraps from the dumpster beside the restaurant. Her search was rewarded by a few limp french fries which she quickly devoured. The woman who spotted the homeless woman exclaimed to her three friends, "Oh, my! Look at that poor woman. I cannot bear to watch this." Then she wiped her mouth, got up from the table, went over, and closed the curtain.

Daily some of us close the curtain on our gospel responsibility. Rather than fighting the poverty around us and abroad, we sometimes choose to turn a blind eye to the problems of the world, problems that we have the resources to help solve. A television report in January 2000, stated that more than 12 million children in the United States alone are affected by hunger. This is a staggering number that should be an embarrassment to Americans with the resources to alleviate the problem. And, of course, this number does not even scratch the surface of hunger worldwide.

If anyone associated with those whom Paul referred to as the lowly, Mother Teresa did. Mother Teresa had a special place in her heart for the poor and those in need, for those who hungered and thirsted after righteousness, and for those who hungered physically. Her attitude here bears a striking contrast to the attitude of some Americans. The late Archbishop John Cardinal O'Connor of New York once remarked, "Contempt of the poor has become a virtue."[9] In other words, some people actually believe the poor are to be despised and feel a responsibility to make their disgust for the poor known. Why is it that we fail to give the poor the benefit of the doubt? Are we so jaded because we see some opportunists taking advantage of the system? Do we fear that money will be taken out of our pockets to put into theirs?

This attitude is similar to the attitude confronted by the prophet Amos in eighth century B.C. Israel. Wealthy landowners, merchants, and leaders had a certain greed and a contempt for the poor, and Amos emerged from his job of shepherding to preach against these injustices. In Amos 5:21 we see God's disdain for those who faithfully held to their religious pomp while ignoring and even abusing the poor (Amos 8:4–6).[10] We *must* consider our own gospel responsibility in this regard, our actions as well as our thoughts and prayers.

Concerning his own missionary work, Paul also coveted the prayers of his brothers and sisters. Read Romans 15:30–31. Do you think Paul is simply requesting the benevolent thoughts of those who know about his work? Do you think he refers to the potential of real danger in the missionary journeys he has planned? He is asking the saints to call upon the power and steadfastness of God to sustain him personally as well as sustain the work in which he is engaged. Like Paul and Teresa, we must gather support and be about the business of ministering to the children of God, regardless of their beliefs, their nationality, or their reasons for need.

Paul ends this chapter with a benediction recounting the power and peace of God. For Paul these are more than words; they are the strength and source of his daily life. He is consumed by the significance of his work and ministry and fully understands the dependence on God and others that such important work implies.

We have a gospel responsibility to be on mission and to support missions. We are not called to do it alone. The sustaining power of the Holy Spirit and the faith influences of our neighbors and communities of faith are there to support us in whatever direction God is calling. Whether we choose to shovel the walk of the neighbor with Alzheimer's, pray for the pastor who serves a church in Taiwan, give our time and money to build Habitat houses, or preach the gospel of joy, hope, and peace to peasants in Russia, the world awaits our faith influence.

Questions for personal reflection

1. Why do you believe poverty exists in the United States and the rest of the world? What is your response to it?

2. Why do you believe there was contempt for the poor in the time of Amos and today?
3. From other accounts you have studied, what do you think were the dangers facing Paul?
4. What does Paul ask for in intercessory prayer? Is God more likely to help people for whom others have prayed rather than people for whom no prayers have been voiced?
5. If you were to ask for intercessory prayer for yourself today, what would you ask an intercessor to pray for?

[1]George Arthur Buttrick, ed., *The Interpreter's Bible* (Nashville: Abingdon Press, 1978), 9:631.
[2]Karl Barth, *The Epistle to the Romans* (London: Oxford University Press, 1933), 524.
[3]Ibid.
[4]Clarence Jordan, *The Cotton Patch Version of Paul's Epistles* (New York: Association Press, 1968), 42
[5]Clifton J. Allen, ed., *The Broadman Bible Commentary* (Nashville: Broadman Press, 1970), 10:272
[6]Ibid., 274.
[7]Jordan, *Cotton Patch Version,* 1968), 44.
[8]Paul J. Achtemeier, *Romans,* vol. in *Interpretation: A Bible Commentary for Teaching and Preaching* (Louisville, KY: John Knox Press, 1985), 229.
[9]Bread for the World Newsletter, January/February 1995, 6.
[10]Ibid.

12

God's Call Brings Triumph, So Give God All the Praise!

What is a woman, just a woman, to do? In her day Lottie Moon met with much opposition from people who didn't think a woman should travel so far on her own to carry the gospel to the people of China. Besides, how would she be received in a world where women were not to teach men or have any kind of authority over them? Lottie's response to this was that if a job needed to be done and she could it, she needed to be about God's business. This brave woman of small physical stature stood head and shoulders above her detractors, those who lacked faith in her ability and authority to minister.

The precedent was set long before the days of Lottie Moon for women to have significant roles in ministry. As we will see in the last chapter of Romans, Paul recognized and appreciated the abilities and the service of men and women alike. No doubt, women were a vital part of his ministry, and all their efforts did not go unnoticed by him.

While some scholars question whether chapter 16 had the same intended destination as the rest of the Book of

Romans,[1] Romans as we have it ends with thanks and encouragement for those who helped Paul in his ministry efforts and showed him kindness. In Romans 16, Paul commends several people by name. Many of those are mentioned nowhere else in the Bible. We know nothing else of their connection to Christ beyond these brief words from Paul.

These names may seem foreign to us and difficult to pronounce. Since we are reading this text many years later, these salutations and remembrances could have little meaning as they name persons with whom we have almost no connection. We may feel a temptation to simply overlook these names, searching instead for something that appears to have more timely significance for us.

Upon further reflection, however, we may discover that these names represent people like many we know, who serve Christ quietly in their own spheres of influence. We could each write our own list of those who have supported us in times of trials and discouragement, as well as those who work with us in Christ's service. Paul has presented us pages from his "photo album" of those with whom he has labored, prayed, suffered, and rejoiced. In his gratitude to each of them, he has specifically mentioned their faithfulness in this letter.

Among the faith influences whom Paul mentions are, again, females and males, Gentiles and Jews. The prominence of women in verses 1–15 is significant here. Nine of the people Paul greets in these verses are women including Prisca, Mary, Junia, Tryphaena, Tryphosa, Persis, the mother of Rufus, Julia, and the sister of Nereus. In addition to those nine women, Paul also mentions in verse 1 Phoebe, who will probably be the courier for this letter to the Romans. For centuries, a portion of this verse, one word in particular, has been mistranslated. The King James Version and many other translations erroneously called Phoebe a servant or a deaconess instead of her true title of deacon. There is nothing to indicate that her role as deacon was in any way different from the role of a male deacon. In fact, we know that she was a significant leader in the church at Cenchreae. Gaventa adds that all of the people listed in Paul's greeting "appear to be engaged in tasks of ministry, a fact that needs to be taken into account in any assessment of the roles of women in early Christianity."[2]

To further elaborate on this mistranslation, Scanzoni and Hardesty write that Paul uses the Greek word referring to Phoebe's title, *diakonos*, 22 times. Eighteen of the 22 times, the King James Version translates the word as "minister," and when referring to Phoebe in verse 1, the King James Version calls her a "servant."[3] Why do you believe those people responsible for the King James Version decided to call Phoebe a servant rather than *deacon?*

One other woman in this list of names bears further mention, Junia. Because she is identified in verse 7 as being prominent among the apostles, many people have speculated that even though Junia was a woman's name, perhaps Paul was referring to a man here. But Scanzoni and Hardesty point out that this debate was cleared up in the fourth century by Chrysostom of Constantinople who said, "Oh, how great is the devotion of this woman that she should be counted worthy of the appellation of apostle!"[4] Paul had tremendous respect for Junia; and while some see her as associating with apostles rather than being an apostle, there is little doubt that her faith influence is quite significant to Paul, and he has great admiration for her ministry.

In the list of names in these verses were those who befriended Paul in his missionary travels, those who supported his work, Christians whose own work brought special affection from Paul, and new Christians who had come to faith in Christ through Paul's ministry. There were also those who had risked their own comfort and safety to help Paul in his work, fellow kinsmen, and fellow prisoners of Paul. While each of these persons may have played a significant role in Paul's ministry, and some like Phoebe were significant church leaders, it is likely that many of them did not play highly visible roles elsewhere. This, of course, does not make their importance to Paul any less valuable. Whether living in the first century or the twenty-first century, people face the temptation to focus on the "stars," or flamboyant leaders. The truth is that those who work quietly and tirelessly toward the common goal accomplish most of the influence and work. They do not expect recognition but seek only the satisfaction that obedience brings.

At my church on All Saints' Day we parade a big banner down the aisle to celebrate the saints of the church. Each person is encouraged to attach a bell to the banner to signify the person, living or deceased, who has been a saint in his or her life. This year I decided to attach a bell for my granddaddy Temples. If you remember, he's that one that I occasionally punched in church when he began to nod off. He was a saint in so many ways, ways that very few people even realized. While not a star or a flamboyant leader, he was significant to me and to those who knew him.

One of the ways I remember his being so saintly and unselfish had to do with his forgiveness of debts. I've heard my mother say that if it had not been for my grandmother, he would have given away everything. He and Grandmama owned and operated West End Grocery on Columbia Avenue in Batesburg, South Carolina, my hometown. The grocery was a little store with blue and orange gas pumps in the front. Granddaddy didn't care what color you were or how much money you had. Everybody was welcomed and everybody got the same good treatment at West End Grocery. He carried soft drinks, bread, hoop cheese, luncheon meat that had to be sliced, liver pudding, canned goods, dipped ice cream, two-for-a-penny cookies, headache powders, loose cigarettes, mullets and mackerels, produce when it was in season, laundry detergent and other cleaning supplies, and candy, lots of candy. Everybody in the community knew and loved Mr. Johnnie. He had a Christlikeness about him that stuck with you, and he always gave you the benefit of the doubt. I remember his constantly asking me, "Tisa Risa, do you know what love is?" And I always said, "What is it, Granddaddy?" He said, "Love. Love is a little hickey shaped like a lizard, runs through your heart and sticks out your gizzard. That's what love is." Later I figured out that what he meant was that love really couldn't be put into words. But he knew what it was, and I know that because I was there.

One day I noticed Granddaddy doing something really strange. I am told that this was not the first time he had done this nor was it the last. He had a huge cardboard box that toilet paper came in, and he was filling it up with these little books. You see, a lot of people bought their groceries from him on credit. He would record their purchases in individual books that were a little bigger than a checkbook. I looked in the cardboard box, and it was at least half full of these credit books, hundreds of them. There is no telling how many thousands of dollars worth of groceries were recorded on the pages of those books, and that was in 1962. I asked, "Granddaddy, what are you gonna do with those?" And he said, "Come on with me." He picked up this heavy, loaded box and we took it out back and set it on fire. Every time I have prayed the Lord's Prayer after that day, when I get to the part about "forgive us our debts, as we forgive our debtors," I think of the day Granddaddy burned the credit books.[5]

This is just one example of one faith influence in my life who was an encouragement and a support to many people. He is probably sitting in heaven with my grandmama right now quite humble and very embarrassed that I am mentioning this, but people like him deserve mention when it comes to this topic. He was just as or even more significant than the most prominent theologian, or Mother Teresa, or Billy Graham, or any of those public figures, at least to me.

Paul's mention of such people in his own life may remind us of many people who have served in similar capacities of support and encouragement. Paul's words also may cause us to reflect upon the ways in which others have served in these roles for us personally, perhaps as a pastor, a church staff member, a teacher, a missionary, another fellow Christian, or maybe even someone who is not a Christian. Likewise, we are to be that support and encouragement to others.

In the New Testament, the *ekklesia* (the church), has three spheres of meaning: Christians in a household, Christians in a city, and Christians in the world. Paul would advise us to pay attention to our support and influence in each of these three realms. In terms of a household and a city, our influence and support can include direct, tangible efforts to minister to those around us. We do this when we mow the lawn of a sick neighbor, call on by telephone or in person one recovering from surgery, prepare a meal at the homeless shelter, visit inmates in the correctional facility, or give blood through the American Red Cross.

While these are concrete ways of lending a hand to those in need, we can also lend support to people we know who are serving others. A simple word of praise or congratulations to someone who has poured her or his heart and soul into a good work goes a long way to affirm that individual's service and to encourage that person to keep up the good work. Again, it is as important here to recognize those on the sidelines just as much and just as often as those in the limelight.

As the sphere enlarges to include the world, our missions activities can still include direct involvement in ministry to those in special need. While we may not be able to go abroad for an extended period of time, life-changing opportunities for short-term service are readily available. We can spend a weekend or a week of vacation helping flood victims who may not be in our immediate communities. We can collect and deliver clothing and medical supplies to Latin American countries ravaged by storms. Even if we are not in a position to physically go to a location in need, our support activities such as prayer and contributions of money and other resources are desperately required.

A former colleague of mine provided an invaluable service to the family members of missionaries through the use of ham, or amateur, radio. In the days when telephone calls abroad were much more expensive, he allowed the two parties to "converse" free of charge on a fairly regular basis. In some cases, the missionary on the field may have lacked access to a telephone, so his radio may have been the best link between the family members. The local family member would come to his house high on a mountain eager to communicate with a loved one in Germany, Nigeria, Taiwan, or Honduras. Imagine the excitement of being able to find out how your brother, daughter, or parents were doing and being able to give news from back home through the use of this radio.

Then, as technology would have it, my colleague's services became all but obsolete. With the advent of email, the people who utilized his services could now communicate with their family members instantaneously practically any time of the night or day. Of course, we're making the big assumption that both parties have access to a computer and email. If we are fortunate enough to enjoy this kind of access, on a daily basis we can send messages of support to people we could otherwise not afford to call. And we don't have to wait days or weeks to get a written response from them through the traditional mail system. The world is changing daily, and who knows how these opportunities will look in the future. Nevertheless, the call to gospel responsibility is the same as it was in Paul's day.

With knowledge of needs around the world and specific individuals who can use our support, the possibilities of direct and indirect service are abundant. All opportunities for learning about world missions strengthen the support we will later give. Once we are informed, we can take action.

Like the two children mentioned earlier, when Nakia was younger, her Sunday School teacher asked the class to write letters to God. At the time at school, Nakia's third-grade class was studying the countries of the world. Very intrigued by the whole idea of a map of the world, Nakia wrote, "Dear God: Who draws the lines around the countries? Love, Nakia."

Faraway countries and how they got to be countries held great interest for Nakia. She wanted information, wanted to understand how the world operates. Africa held special interest for Nakia because she had been told that most of her ancestors had come from that continent. Gaining this understanding of places outside our own backdoor is crucial, especially in a time when the world is getting more and more connected and we have immediate access to events around the globe. Now more than ever, children should be encouraged at an early age to think about people and places that may look different but hold incredible wonder and possibilities for both giving and receiving.

As a young GA in a Baptist church, missions, of course, had a strong emphasis. At the age of about 9 or

10 I remember working on my Forward Steps with Myra Beth Senterfeit whom I have already mentioned in two previous chapters. Recently when I was at my parents' home for the holidays, I ran across a decades-old picture of Myra and me sitting at the kitchen table. I was wearing my Camp Rawls GA shirt (which was about two sizes too large) and we were memorizing the following which I still remember verbatim: "Knowing that countless people grope in darkness and giving attention to his commands, I assert my allegiance to Jesus Christ, to his church and its activities." We also memorized a series of things we were to do as GAs, which still happens to be a pretty good list: "Attempting with God's help to abide in him through prayer, to advance in wisdom by Bible study, to acknowledge my stewardship of time, money, and personality, to adorn myself with good works, and to accept the challenge of the Great Commission."

That litany of allegiance has stuck with me since I was 9 years old. While I have not always been faithful to the promises and their gospel responsibilities, I have been affected by them. These words served and serve as a significant faith influence in my life. A part of that GA influence was the ever-present map of the world at every meeting I ever attended. Kids at school complained that it wasn't fair that those Baptist GA girls always knew the answers in geography class. My GA sisters were never at a loss for recognizing and locating nearly every country in the world, at least the ones where we had missionaries. We had had good training. Every night we read in the back of *Tell* magazine (forerunner of *Discovery*) the names of missionaries who had birthdays that day and prayed for them by name. The magazine also listed the job they did and the country where they served.

Years later when that GA shirt would have fit better, I worked at that same Woman's Missionary Union camp in South Carolina. As in my childhood, that world map was a permanent fixture. Each night, one cabin was responsible for presenting the prayer calendar, and each girl was given a piece of paper bearing the name of a birthday missionary and the country where he or she served. The paper was in the shape of a star, a candle, a lightbulb, or something to remind us that these missionaries were significant faith influences. A piece of tape was stuck to the back of the paper, and each girl was to go up to the microphone, read the name of the missionary and the country of service, and stick the paper on the correct country on the map. As you know, some of the names of those countries are a bit hard to pronounce, especially for 8- or 9-year-olds. One evening after supper I was helping cabin 3 practice for this prayer calendar presentation. A little girl named Jill, 9, decided to give a helpful hint to her cabin mates. She told them, "If you get up there and forget how to pronounce the name of the place, just say Japan. That's where most of the missionaries are from anyway. Besides, God will know how to find them."

Jill was not exactly accurate in her assessment of missionary distribution around the world, but she did probably help alleviate a little bit of anxiety. She also pointed out that God can work despite our failings. But the point here is that the exposure to the work of missionaries around the United States and the rest of the world served as valuable training and a tremendous faith influence for all those little girls. Many of them began to wonder how God would use them.

Perhaps we need to examine a lesson we can learn from these bright-eyed, eager little girls who seek God's will for their lives. All along the way many of them have learned of the joys, rewards, and responsibilities of ministry in the name of Jesus. They listen with interest to the words of teachers, pastors, and missionaries (male and female) who tell of God's work all over the world. Lottie Moon is not just an offering to them; they know who she was and what she did. These impressionable girls are told to listen to where God is calling them and to what type of service. "You can be anything God calls you to be," they are told. Like the support Paul received from so many friends and fellow ministers, these girls and young women deserve the same support and encouragement when God calls them to service in the name of Christ, including avenues of service once they have responded affirmatively to God's call.

Questions for personal reflection

1. List each person Paul names in Romans 16:1–5; then list a characteristic of each, if possible, from the clues in these verses.
2. In what ways do some of these people remind you of some of your supportive friends?
3. How might we become more informed about ways in which we can be of support, encouragement, and service in the world?

Called to close fellowship and to triumph over evil

Paul ends the first section of chapter 16 with the admonition to "greet one another with a holy kiss" (v. 16). Jesus' disciples practiced this custom of the Jewish rabbis. As the custom became part of early Christian worship, it reinforced the Christian principles of absence of formality, social distinctions, and discrimination. Rich and poor, male and female, Jew and Gentile alike got the same greeting. The "holy kiss" reflected true fellowship based on the love of Christ. Such affection and closeness would certainly produce the following kind of harmony.

After lengthy references to those who played meaningful roles in his ministry, Paul makes a strong statement to the Christians at Rome to remain harmonious and steadfast in the truth. Read carefully Romans 16:17–20. Apparently, Paul connects Christian fellowship to unity. In verses 17–18, Paul picks up on that same topic highlighted in chapters 14–15 by cautioning against divisions that prohibit such unity. Speaking of the sly ones in these verses, Clarence Jordan says, “Shun them like the plague, for such gentlemen are not committed to our Lord Christ but to their own welfare. With their smooth sermons and pious prayers they captivate the minds of the immature.”[6] Paul reminds the early Christians to remain true to their faith despite what they may hear from these smooth talkers. *Koinonia,* or fellowship, strengthens faithfulness and helps us avoid these pitfalls that come our way. Christians can more easily overcome temptation and evil when the faithfulness of many reinforces the faithfulness of the individual.

Paul admonishes the Romans to be aware of the subtleties of evil. Even though he expresses confidence in their faithfulness, he reminds them that victory over evil will come only through their obedience and faith in Christ. As in the earlier chapters of Romans, evil is personified through Paul’s reference to Satan in verse 20, and Paul points out that Satan has met his match with God.

Called to stability and glory, to spread the gospel to all nations

The first half of this last chapter of Romans includes instructions to greet and thank a variety of people who had benefited and helped Paul in numerous ways. In verses 21–23, Paul includes greetings from other Christians along with his *amanuensis,* or secretary, Tertius, who was employed to write this letter. Paul's inclusion of so many people in chapter 16 shows his understanding of the importance of cooperation and fellowship and his generous attitude towards others which is crucial for the unity that he seeks.[7]

The chapter ends with a doxology to the praise of Christ. Called a "floating doxology" because of its appearance in three different places in various manuscripts,[8] this doxology is intended to end the letter to the church at Rome. Considered to be one of the great benedictions in biblical literature, in these few verses Paul manages to summarize succinctly the major aspects of all 16 chapters in Romans. We are to celebrate God's wondrous grace-filled plan realizing that all strength will come from obedience and faithfulness to the gospel of Christ. His birth, life, death, and resurrection offer abundant living for all—to Jews and Gentiles who were the subject of most of the Book of Romans as well as to all nations. In places as far away as Bosnia or as near as Birmingham, we are responsible for spreading this saving gospel message; and if necessary, to use words.

Our gifts and talents for sharing the love of Christ differ radically from person to person. By using those gifts, we are exercising our gospel responsibility, listening and responding to God and acting as change agents in the world. Nothing we do to act as God's hands, feet, and voice is ever a small thing.

I still have that GA shirt from Camp Rawls. The green and gold colors have faded, but I can still read all the words. I kept that shirt for nearly 35 years for many reasons, and all the reasons were significant faith influences. It reminds me of my mother who washed the daylights out of that shirt so that I could wear it almost every day. It reminds me of my grandmother Lewis who, blind from diabetes, hummed hymns constantly and died the year that I bought that shirt. It reminds me of Scrappy Wherry who led our GA group and encouraged us with those Forward Steps. It reminds me of Mrs. Corder back at my home church who wrote a note to me that summer so that I would get mail at camp. It reminds me of Mrs. Harriet Crapps who took all my little Baptist buddies and me in her Sunday School class under her wing, into her home, and to the beach. It reminds me of Betsy, the lifeguard at the camp who took an interest in a gawky 9-year-old. It reminds me of Pearl Johnson, a camp missionary who gave me a Bible marker that she had signed and brought all the way from Japan (really Japan!). And it reminds me of Lottie Moon who did not let adversity and opposition stand in her way of service. I am thankful for all of those faith influences and many more who taught us in so many different ways what gospel responsibility involves and how we should respond.

The world is a much different place than it was when I bought that shirt, but the Great Commission is still the same. Maybe in some small way through the love of Christ and the guidance of the Holy Spirit we too will become faith influences toward gospel responsibility in this changing world. So what *is* a woman, just a woman, to do? The possibilities are limitless.

Questions for personal reflection

1. List the evils Paul notes in Romans 16:17–20. Which ones pertain to you?
2. As you rely on the Holy Spirit, how will you show your willingness to obey in these areas?
3. How does Romans 16:25–27 apply to your life?
4. In what ways, big and small, are you a faith influence? In what ways do you desire to become more of a faith influence?

[1]Paul J. Achtemeier, *Romans,* vol. in *Interpretation: A Bible Commentary for Teaching and Preaching* (Louisville, KY: John Knox Press, 1985), 233–35.
[2]Beverly Roberts Gaventa, "Romans," in *The Women's Bible Commentary,* ed. Carol A. Newsom and Sharon H. Ringe (Louisville, KY: Westminster/John Knox Press, 1992), 320.
[3]Letha Dawson Scanzoni and Nancy A. Hardesty, *All We Are Meant to Be* (Nashville: Abingdon Press, 1986), 80.
[4]Chrysostom, *The Homilies of St. John Chrysostom*, Nicene and Post Nicene Fathers, First Series (Grand Rapids: William B. Eerdmans Publishing Company, 1956), 11:555, quoted in Scanzoni and Hardesty, *All We Are Meant to Be,* 81.
[5]Tisa Lewis, "Spiritual Confessions of a Searching Boomer" (working title; unpublished manuscript), 123.
[6]Clarence Jordan, *The Cotton Patch Version of Paul's Epistles* (New York: Association Press, 1968), 45.
[7]Achtemeier, *Romans,* 238–39.
[8]Clifton J. Allen, ed., *The Broadman Bible Commentary* (Nashville: Broadman Press, 1970), 10:285.

Epilogue

All my life I have enjoyed telling stories, some true and some not so true! Unfortunately, I am not quite as skilled at this as Aunt Emmons and Uncle Marvin, two of the best storytellers I have ever known. Stories for me bring to life facts and ideas in a way that little else can. Most of us as children perked up whenever we heard the words, "Once upon a time . . ." Emmons and Marvin didn't even need to use these words to let us know that they were about to tell a good one.

In her delightful, encyclopedic book, *Storytelling in Religious Education,* my friend Susan Shaw presents a comprehensive, practical look at of the importance of stories in our lives. She tells us that the Christian story cannot be told fully by any one person, not even Paul. Because our experiences are limited, we must listen to others' experiences and interpretations of the way the gospel has worked in their lives. Their stories can serve as our faith influences and enrich our lives.[1]

Our theology or what we believe about God and how God relates to persons cannot be separated from our biography. Who we are and what we have experienced influence our faith in ways we cannot even imagine. Cassie's ideas about God and the church were greatly influenced by the Ku Klux Klan members of her church. Nakia's biblical interpretations were influenced by the hours of discussion with her family around the kitchen table. My positive images of God no doubt have their early roots in the love and care shown by my parents and grandparents.

Faith influences us in ways that are beyond our comprehension. Faith influences differ radically from person to person. Paul was greatly influenced by the culture in which he lived. Children in Sweden describe God as a blue-eyed blonde, and Italian children see God as much darker. We often see God in our own image and no one of us has the complete story, only glimpses of grace and glory. Each of us is put here to contribute a chapter, to be a faith influence. We do not understand all the mysteries of God. But we each have a story with a little *s*, and we do know a Story with a capital *S*—a Story of Peace and Light.

Remember Janie, my friend and faith influence, the missionary? I said that I was amazed and excited that I could communicate with her oceans apart by email any time for free. The news that is even better than that is we have even more convenient access to God. Patiently God waits to hear from us and for us to listen to that still, small voice that calls us to gospel responsibility, no modem required.

[1]Susan Shaw, *Storytelling in Religious Education* (Birmingham: Religious Education Press, 1999), 83–84.

About the author

Tisa Lewis is associate professor of human development and Christian education at Montreat College in Montreat, North Carolina. She holds a BS in biology from the University of South Carolina and an MA and a PhD in Christian education from Southern Baptist Theological Seminary. Her hobbies include golf, movies, and filmmaking.

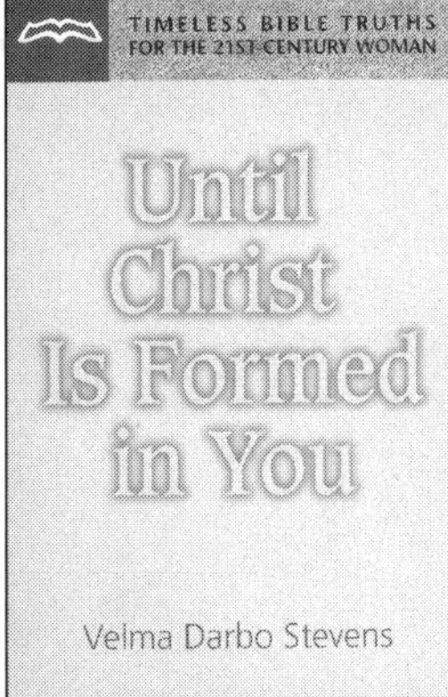

If you enjoyed this book, you will also enjoy *Until Christ Is Formed in You* and *Women of Faith.*

Available by calling WMU Customer Service at 1-800-968-7301, and by visiting the WMU Web site at www.wmu.com.